TO OBEY IS TO REIGN

To obey is to reign

The Beauty and Grandeur of the Religious Life

By F. X. RONSIN, S.J.

Translated from the French by
SISTER EUGENIA LOGAN, S.P.
Saint Mary-of-the-Woods, Indiana

ST. PAUL PUBLICATIONS
NEW YORK - CANFIELD - DERBY - BOSTON

NIHIL OBSTAT
    Charles E. Ross, J.C.L.
        Censor deputatus

IMPRIMATUR
    ✛ Paul Schulte, D.D.
        Archbishop of Indianapolis

Indianapolis, Indiana
February 18, 1961

Library of Congress Catalog Card Number 61-14113

To Senior Religious, evaluating the wisdom of their choice,

To Newly Professed, embarking on a magnificent adventure

To Young People, seeking for a beautiful use of their lives,

To Upright Souls, aware of the sincerity of a testimony.

TABLE OF CONTENTS

FOREWORD

There are probably more than a million religious women in the Church.* In view of the various ways of looking at things, very diverse conclusions could be drawn from such figures. Some people might let themselves be misled by the poverty of the results and might expect more good to be effected, but faith as well as experience has confirmed us in optimism.

The works of God can never be failures.

The Church of Christ is holy.

Catholic sanctity effects the most beautiful and the most striking triumphs of the human soul, raised by God to moral beauty and greatness.

The religious life should be judged more by its successes than by its failures.

To these theoretical reasons, we bring our humble experience. During our forty years of the apostolate, we have conversed with a hundred religious families. By the thousands, we have met consecrated persons belonging to five continents. We have known their failures, even their trials; the most elementary loyalty forces one to acknowledge this.

* At the end of 1957, the most recent statistical data gives 270,00 (Priests and Brothers together) and 1,000,000 religious women.

On the other hand, we have come back marveling at the moral splendors we have seen. We have heard accounts of admirable lives; of thirty and forty years of absolute dedication, simple and persevering through the years with never a regret unless it be for not having done enough for God or for not having devoted themselves more to their brethren.

Apostles of every country and of all dioceses could, by the hundreds, bring testimony of the same kind.

No—the Kingdom of God is not a land of fancy, impossible to find and to explore. It is an intensely living realm; it flourishes under our very eyes. The souls of the elect people it. What a favor to have been able to dwell so long among these fortunate ones! The book you are about to read is not only a resume of a lived experience, it is the faithful echo of thousands of gathered testimonies.

Our religious lives are beautiful: they are veritable pilgrimages toward the splendor of God. They are great things because they participate in the greatness of the Master we serve.

The spirit of poverty brings to us many freedoms. It restores to us the souls of children. Thanks to it, we should seek out the victims of poverty in order to share sincerely in their sufferings.

Chastity magnifies our love, giving us as our friends: God, Jesus Christ, and the Blessed Virgin. It puts in the hearts of many religious such a maternal love that they often surpass mothers according to the flesh in devotedness and heroism.

They follow Christ, the King of the obedient. In the school of the handmaid of the Lord, the modern religious, through the vow of obedience, benefits all the victims of human servitude, from slaves of former times to those of our present generation.

The common life gives us superiors who are often very kind. The Divine Will is clearly shown us by our Rule. In adapting ourselves to all its demands, we try to come to the assistance of those who suffer in difficult or torturing types of work.

Fraternal charity frees us in general from prejudices and party opinions. It aids us to see and love, in every human being, a child of God.

Persevering prayer leads us to the country of divine light. Prayer gives us the spirit of praise and a solicitude for all the blessings it sends. Through it, we may become before God the advocates of our brethren, of sinners, or of unbelievers.

Oppressed by the sadness of the world, our sick, helpless, and suffering religious should become, day after day, more compassionate for the physical and moral sufferings of the sorrowful people of all countries. We seek to reveal to the most unfortunate of our brethren our conviction of the grandeur of suffering.

God and the Church are our masters and our guides in the apostolate. Our supplications and our apostolic ventures range from individual conversions to world-wide, even cosmic views.

For those who do not believe enough in the marvelous destiny of the human soul, it would be profitable to reflect on the thousands of souls transformed by love of God and love of their fellowmen.

The cry of St. Teresa of Avila could be uttered again in our day: "What would become of the world without religious?"

We thank in advance all the European and American publishers who have offered to bring out translations of this the latest of our books.

F.X.R.

Poitiers, Jan. 1, 1960

CHAPTER I

BEAUTY AND GRANDEUR OF THE RELIGIOUS LIFE

> "God sends His light upon us as
> we approach Him. To serve Him
> makes us Kings. . . ."
>
> Saint Leo

Our lives are beautiful: they are a progress toward the splendor of God. They are grand because "to serve God makes us Kings." [1]

Made to the likeness of the Creator of beauty, the human soul aspires to beauties ever more glorious. Man turns to beauty as flowers turn toward light. Unwearied and unsatisfied, the searchers for beauty trudge on, but, in their journey, all do not go forward at the same rate. Some stop too soon, contenting themselves with material beauties, the only things that in a degree satisfy their desires.

Far happier are they who, beyond the beauty of color, of flowers, and of faces, discover the incomparable world of the splendor of souls—the last stage toward the beauty of God. Made beautiful on the divine heights, as was Moses on Sinai,[2] they show forth to others and for the benefit of humanity some reflections of the splendor of God. His all-powerful beauty has purified them, freed and transfigured them. One of the missions of religious in this modern world is to make themselves apostles and propagators of the beauty of God.

Drawn by the all-beautiful God, our souls apply themselves zealously to the service of His majesty. Challenges stimulate us. In every country and in every century thousands of persons have dignified the expression, "to serve."

Even today, science, leaders, and causes are served with enthusiasm. Dreams of excelling urge on our contemporaries. Although we are incapable of doing more than they are doing, we dream of excelling them in the quality of our work. One persevering *ascesis* will aid us to purify our service, to extend it into domains and connections where the majority of human beings scarcely ever dream of carrying theirs.

The service of our brethren will be only an application of our service of God, Who is so great a Master that He has in relation to us only rights. In becoming constant, complete, and universal our service will allow us to surpass the great multitude of those who serve. Thus it is that in serving God, one reaches the most enviable of "royalties."

I. BEAUTY OF RELIGIOUS LIVES

From the humble violet to the splendor of God there is displayed a panorama of beauty.

The human being can be enchanted by material beauty in its hundred forms, but it has the privilege of being able to explore the universe of souls.

One can say: "Even despite the fall of Adam, the world remains a marvel." [3] From insects to stars, everything is beautiful in it. And when Almighty God draws beings from nothingness, He proclaims the triumph of His work.

"And God saw that it was good . . ." [4] is the familiar

refrain of the praise of the Creator. From the infinitesimal atom to the infinitely great, all is admirable in the work of our Father. Religious are profoundly aware of their brothers, the scientists. Explorers, pioneers, dedicated researchers, make known marvels of a fascinating nature. Discoverers of unknown and unsuspected worlds, in some way they aid the "professionals" of prayer to chant with an increased appreciation and better informed praise, the canticle, "Benedicite, omnia opera Domini Domino. . . ." "O you creatures of God, proclaim His glory." [5]

Happily for us, there are not lacking religious capable of revealing to their less educated sisters the beautiful things which they have seen through their research miscroscopes. They tell them that the world of snow crystals alone has a fascination which has filled some lives.[6] There are kinds of rock which, by the extreme delicacy of their fossils, enable us to admire the mysterious forms of life even though they were formed in ages far off from our times.

To simple and pure religious souls, naturally in accord with beauty, no guide is needed to open to them the world of varied flowers and butterflies in the bright sunlight. By themselves they could discover and appreciate the innumerable varieties of birds, the chorus of their songs, and the extraordinary gorgeousness of their plumage.

God alone knows the number of consecrated souls who have already supplicated Him to recompense, as He knows how to do, the boldness of the adventurers who reveal to us the wonders of the submarine world. The first discoveries are promising! A specialist in sea coral tells us that

"Nature submerged in the sea is as beautiful if not more so than nature risen to our view. . . ." [7]

There are pure dawns on eternal snows; unforgettable sunsets across the calm of oceans. How many religious know how to enjoy such serene sights! They never forget that Saint Francis of Assisi sang his famous Canticle to the Sun.

In their turn, artists, passionate followers of all forms of beauty, do their utmost to lead us farther, themselves guided by the most exalted of their dreams. It is generally agreed that the unsurpassed wonders remain the temples, raised to the glory of the divinity. From the Pyramids of Egypt to the Temple of Angkor, from the Parthenon to the Cathedrals of all Christendom, the builders of genius encourage souls on their journey to God.

In the ascending hierarchy of beauty, at the top-most point of the world of physical creation, the human being stands in triumph. The sculptors of Chartres did not hesitate to immortalize in stone the precise moment when the God of beauty dreamed of making man to His own image.

The beauty of souls

We understand very well those whom material beauty delights, as well as those who are enamored by the beauty of faces; but beyond all these temporary enjoyments doomed to perish, we know that there exists a wondrous universe of souls, in which adornments shine forth in proportion to the progress towards the splendor of God. Wise men and saints agree in assuring us that it is through the soul that one enters the country of ever-increasing and lasting beauty.

"The lover of thy body, when its flower is shed, leaves you." [8]

"To love the body, even adorned with beauty and graces
. . . is to love nothing; it is trying to hold an ever-fleeing
shadow." [9]

"Apply therefore, said Socrates, all your strength and
heart to make for yourselves the most beautiful soul
possible." [10]

Many religious are ignorant of this formula although they
have already adopted this program. For twenty, thirty, forty
years they have striven to model themselves on God. The
results of their struggles unwearyingly carried on adorn their
souls with beauties steadily more beneficial to the people
about them. One of the marvels of the Church is the whole
army of religious on the march toward the beauty of God.

"O God, Thou Whose greatness, majesty, and glory
clothe Thee like a vesture, Whose cloak is the sun!" [11]

Purifications and discoveries

These efforts toward divine beauty begin in a with-
drawing from ugliness. When one has been the witness of
so much poverty, weakness, and vileness, one begins to
dream of the purity of God, the most beautiful Guest Who
dwells unsleeping in our hearts, and the longing for His
purity stirs in us. We feel then how much pettiness and narrowness are merely human, and the desire grows to escape
from narrowing horizons.

Novices bring from the world a common enough assort-
ment of limitations and prejudices. Each one has his own
share of defects and faults. Self-mastery is not yet fully

tested. Soon enough a great confidence awakens in their youthful hearts. It is enough for them to look toward their elders to understand that in them virtues already acquired are only the reflections of the divine attributes, and that patience, mildness, forbearance, benevolence, are possible things. The evidence shows the many touches of God Who leaves on His creatures the imprint of the hands of a moulder, marvelous in purity.

Learning the beauty of God

Knowing that good will and human efforts, even aided by a certain degree of grace, do not go very far in the laborious ascent, and that all this will not lead one to the summit of the mountain of perfection, it is on God alone that one relies to embellish souls by reflections of His own beauty. The end as well as the recompense of our lives is to study and to contemplate in order to clothe ourselves steadily with the eternal light which transfigures.

The soul in contemplation, facing the Infinite Beauty, is a ready canvas offered to the Divine Painter. It is a mirror, anxious to be able to reflect the face of God. When one believes with all one's strength in the meeting and in the efficacy of desires in perfect balance: that of a sincere soul anxious to purify itself of the last blemishes of its ugliness, and that of the source of beauty itself seeking always in creatures an increasing likeness to it, then we can imagine, without fully realizing it, all the power of transfiguration flowing from God into fervent souls. All this takes place in the silence of morning prayer, in thanksgivings filled with desires and appeals. It is the certain and visible result of the Office chanted so many times. These souls cannot praise the glory of God and supplicate Him indefinitely without someday being overwhelmed by torrents of beauty.

It cannot be in vain that religious in the prayer of Prime [12] supplicate their Father to illuminate their whole being. The Collect of the Vigil of Pentecost stresses and dwells upon the daily morning appeal:

> "O God, hear our suppliant prayers. May the splendor of our Lord God come upon us and let shine the splendor of Thy light dazzling our whole being. And may the Holy Spirit, the splendor of Thy glory, illumine and regenerate the souls of those who are entering upon the true way."

Propagators of the beauty of God

Why are we lacking in daring? Let us not hesitate to bring ourselves to the paternal and great views of God for His children. Material creation, obedient to its law, shows the beauty with which its Creator has endowed it. Souls are still better fitted to transmit to us some reflections of the splendor of God. As the Father chooses some saints to reincarnate and make perceptible His infinite goodness, so He confides to others the mission of making the refulgence of His beauty penetrate into the hearts of people. The friends of Christ and of the Immaculate Virgin remain the most faithful mirrors of the divine glory. In order to convince men that His beauty can be assimilated, even by themselves, God has used the souls of the saints to send out to masses of people some rays of His light. The dazzling world of our saints is like a majestic rainbow breaking up its brilliance, the beauty of God, among mankind. One of the missions of religious persons at present living their ideals in the

Church, is to prove to this generation that they are faithful
mirrors of their Heavenly Father.

Invested with the same beauty, souls become fraternal

Shining with the same light, bearers of a beauty emanating from the same source, souls become alike and fraternal.
Among those who are the children of God age, rank, and
title do not count. We are surprised sometimes at the success of certain religious with their pupils and their evident
ascendancy over young people. We forget that the beauty
of God Who dwells in them becomes a marvelous bond of
union with their pupils.

Primary classes

In the primary classes it becomes evident that God gathers
together and harmonizes souls by the regenerating effect of
His light. The countenance of aged religious differs only in
imperceptible ways from that of the youngest children. The
eyes of both carry reflections of the simplicity, of the clear-
ness of God. In touch with the youngest of the human family,
these old teachers believe no longer in the malice of other
persons, so familiar have they become with innocence so
near to the splendor of the Heavenly Father. Religious at
the end of their lives and the smallest children speak to one
another the language of Paradise.

Women educators

These irreplaceable beginnings leave their mark for life
on the souls of youth. Some women will preserve throughout

a long life, and in spite of all the moral dangers they may
come in contact with, the understanding of moral grandeur,
of the beauty of souls which have become familiar with
God. Living in virtue, in simplicity and constancy, religious
imprint these virtues on the flexible souls of youth like the
seal which leaves a faithful impression on hot wax.

Benefiting the masses

We wonder sometimes how reflections of the splendor of
God could penetrate into the "shadows," where live masses
of wretched people and where the weak and those defeated
by life dwell in moral destitution. Let us never forget that
the great God remains the friend of the humble. As an ordinary thing, it is from among the little ones that He is pleased
to choose His ambassadors for the most important missions.
From David the shepherd to the shepherdess of Bartrés, from
the infant Samuel to the humble Carmelite of Lisieux, we
find this characteristic of the divine law. From the world
of obscure religious, God recruits those who will carry His
beauty to the hearts of multitudes of little ones.

Hospital and Visiting Nurses

Aware of the greatness of the mission they have received,
the child-like messengers know they can count on the help
of the Father Who sends them. Their apostolic ambitions
expand to a country or a continent. And the God of beauty
will use the triumphs obtained in the souls of His consecrated
ones to bring confidence to many people of good will in their
quest for moral splendor. Too many disappointing experiences have made them sceptical. Then an illness or an acci-

dent suddenly shows them, through the religious nurses, a world hitherto totally unknown to them. Or perhaps on the street a chance but happy encounter has been a sudden revelation of kindness, understanding, and dedication in the gentle countenance of a sincere religious totally devoted to God and her fellowmen. It is to that day, to that precise moment, that some converts trace their return to the Kingdom. . . . If they were to go back over the path they have traveled, they would mark it thus: God is good because at this place He opened out a human life and made it aspire higher until it reached a splendor which transfigures.

The extent of victory

The multiplicity as well as the importance of their victories never astonish the humble and faithful propagators of the beauty of God. Blindly trusting in the goodness and power of their Father, they know Him to be generous and lavish in renewing for the benefit of the souls of apostles the magnificent gesture by which He benefitted the chosen and preferred people of long ago.

"And thy renown went forth among the nations for thy
beauty, for thou wast perfect through my beauty which
I put upon thee, saith the Lord God.[13]

Behold one of the solid bases upon which our reasonable optimism rests. Throughout the Church, humble religious, daughters of all races of the earth, endeavor for the benefit of this generation, to show forth multiple aspects of the beauty of God. They prove to all those hungry for an ideal, for virtue, and for moral splendor that the plan and the "dream" of God have been followed during the centuries. Our Church remains the great marvel, and on its vast panorama of loveliness its innumerable religious

> "form the race that seeks for Him, that seeks the face of the God of Jacob." [14]

> "O Thou Who art the light, Thou the splendor!"

> "Resplendent you come, O powerful One, from the everlasting mountains." [15]

II. OUR RELIGIOUS LIVES ARE GREAT, BECAUSE "TO SERVE GOD MAKES US KINGS"

Fallen man keeps a longing for beauty; he preserves a very keen consciousness of greatness. The passion for "serving" sweeps the elite of nations toward the sublime.

Our generation, amazed and breathless, observes the gigantic and killing efforts put forth by thousands of scientists in every country to conquer diseases, one after another; to alleviate, to some degree, the great suffering of men.

Confronted by this permanent struggle, religious feel themselves roused to a fraternal emulation. They recognize honestly that they cannot surpass their human brothers in their unremitting efforts. They must, then, put forth their strength in a constant uplifting struggle, to purify and free that struggle from all self-interest, but above all make it as completely and universally for God as they can.

Two ways remain open to them to attain royalty in God's service: among the number of those who serve, they will endeavor to become the very best; and totally and absolutely devoted to the greatest of Masters, their service "makes them Kings."

Service

In every language spoken by men, the expression "to serve" has many meanings. It calls to mind a great race of slaves and victims of every form of human servitude. On the other hand, among all the races of the earth, each generation transmits to the one that replaces it the word SERVICE with all its connotations indefinitely enriched.

Whether they serve their country, their people, great causes, or beloved leaders, men do it with a passion which elevates and makes them great. God alone can count the number of lives offered and sacrificed to such ideals.

Today, and throughout the world, it is perhaps the sciences which gather the greatest number of researchers and pioneers and enthusiastic servants. Like all other great causes, science has its casualties and its martyrs. It demands of its followers an unremitting and thoroughly disinterested toil.

When, toward the end of 1898, Pierre and Marie Curie put the finishing touches on the work of isolating the first bit of radium, they worked under hardships, taking only brief and improvised meals. They shortened their sleep considerably. At the time of this brilliant achievement, they knew that by patenting their discovery they could become millionaires. That view was immediately set aside through a very fine and disinterested consideration: "It would be contrary to the scientific spirit."

Pasteur and many other noteworthy discoverers of genius were not looking for wealth. Some of them died in destitution, but often also with the joy of being able to arrest disease, to alleviate sorrow, or to lessen the physical sufferings of their poor fellowmen. In 1955 when Alexander Fleming, one of the "discoverers" of penicillin died, the entire world press rendered him a solemn tribute. Thanks to him, persons by the millions had escaped death. It was a recompense beyond measure, much better than a gigantic fortune.

Going beyond the goal

Ambition and the hope of further successes will never cease to exist in the hearts of men. A man of genius who has produced a masterpiece will endeavor twenty times more to surpass it. We recognize this through having heard so often the statement made by the champions of all countries: "The next time I hope to do still better." At the close of the Olympic Games it is customary to check all records beaten. In 1956, at the Olympic at Melbourne, they counted up 58 of them. One of the successes was that of the Mimoun, who had competed for twelve years before winning the Marathon.

Fraternal emulation

How then can religious, in their fraternal emulation, ever succeed in surpassing their brothers in their humane efforts? It seems to them materially impossible to use any more energy, or to devote more time to work. Delcasse said—and that as early as 1900—"Whoever does not work fourteen hours a day is a lazy fellow." [16]

An ascesis makes souls great

It is in other fields and through other methods that consecrated souls attempt to glorify their sovereign Master by serving Him. There is a world in which we have opportunities of winning victories less showy but more complete and definitive than those which scientists can pride themselves upon. They are masters of matter, whose mysterious forces they have succeeded in calculating and "governing," but even the greatest devotees of science have not all been able to dominate their own passions. There are some who cannot suppress their resentment. Others remain powerless to set aside prejudice and even deep-seated hatreds until death.

Besides their work, and beyond the long hours given to their brethren, the loving servants of the sovereign Master surrender to Him the domains of their senses, faculties, and heart. Each morning we say at Prime:

"O Lord God Almighty, Who hast safely brought us to the beginning of this day, let Thy powerful grace so conduct us through it that we may not fall into any sin, but that all our words, thoughts, and works may be guided by the rules of Thy heavenly justice. . . ." [17]

It is to make us realize better this wish and this program that Saint Ignatius of Loyola proposes to us this prayer:

"Take, O Lord, and receive my liberty, my memory, my intelligence, and all my will; all that I possess you have given me. To You, O Lord, I return it. All is Yours." [18]

The efforts and struggles are carried on without relaxation, obstinately, with a persistence sometimes heroic, as long as one faculty or another has not been completely immolated to the control of God. Louise de la Valliere, in Carmel,

Sister Louise of Mercy, has given the account of the last and most difficult of her victories.

"Through the goodness (of God) my heart is detached and my will tends only to what pleases Him, but that importunate memory which I have desired to put far from me . . . wages against me eternal combats. There is nothing else to be destroyed. I ask God to complete His work." [19]

These battles are very much hidden, this service not striking enough to be hailed by the multitude. We know that God wills this and that He loves our struggles. They are the things that help to throw open by "violence" the narrow door of the Kingdom.[20]

Competition in our dedication

Our dedication to our brethren, as constant and complete as it can be, puts us in competition with all the friends of men. We dare to affirm that human beings are better loved and served by religious families than by any other persons who are concerned with their distress.

We are doing only elementary justice in admiring and praising the conscientiousness and devotion of physicians towards all the sufferers of the world. A common and superb ideal sustains them in their wearisome struggles to conquer a disease, to alleviate a pain, to restore the mental balance of an individual, to save a threatened life at any cost. Doctors by the thousands have sacrificed their own lives in such incessant and worldwide contests.

Less known and celebrated, religious can also count

throughtout the world a great number of victims of charity. Above all, being instruments of the love of the God Who dwells in them, they surround the afflicted with a service more universal, more total. To see, in a human being, a person to be respected, a life to be saved, is enough to arouse heroism in the medical corps and the admirable staff which assists it. But to see in a poor child the image of God Himself, to know how to discover His presence in it, widens and transfigures the gift of one's self to the sick. Nursing communities have long meditated upon, assimilated, and lived such texts as these: The body of the patient

> "should be like the body of Jesus . . . of whom you touch the flesh and the members . . . Jesus is made tangible in the person." [21]

Cancer or leprosy can ravage and disfigure faces. Even among the most unrecognizable of our brethren, the religious finds without too much effort, the "divine Leper" of Calvary.[22] Happy the wounded and the tortured whose wounds are dressed by the pure hands of her who "venerates" in their bodies the flesh of her God.

God must be first served

The complete and loving service to our brothers is a simple and logical application of our service of God. God is so fully our Master that He has over us only rights, and He has all of them, even that of making us slaves full of love for our fellowmen. Texts dealing with the transcendence of God are familiar to us. They help to put into our hearts such a sense of His greatness, of His demands, and of His rights that we serve this King unconditionally, and without any hope whatever of an earthly recompense.

"He is our Master and He is our God and our Father." [23]

". . . There is no God else beside Me." [24]

"For the Lord of all shows no partiality, nor does He fear greatness, because He Himself made the great as well as the small . . ." [25]

Under His gaze

". . . the whole world is nothing but a drop of dew shining on the grass in the morning." [26]

And let us listen to the commentaries which Saint Teresa of Avila has left us on these passages, so long meditated upon with love:

"O absolute Master of the universe, Thou art the power which nothing can resist, the ocean of goodness, wisdom personified. Thou art the Eternal with limitless perfections, the unfathomable abyss of marvels. Thou, the plenitude and the source of all beauty, and again, infinite strength. I would wish to gather together in my own being all the eloquence and the wisdom contained in every human heart. Then I would wish it to be possible here below, where perhaps our knowledge is so poor, to cast one ray of light on one of your perfections, which it has never been given to anyone to analyze. O Thou my Lord and my Good." [27]

Following this hymn on the grandeur of God, uttered by one of the greatest religious women of all times, it is easier for us to accept the incomparable conclusion which she draws from it.

> "His Majesty has been, for me, a veritable book in which I saw all truth. Blessed be such a Book, which leaves behind an impression of what is read therein and in such a way that it cannot be forgotten." [28]

More than ever convinced of the rights and demands of such a God, let us adopt the principle of David:

> "I must not offer to the Lord holocausts which cost me nothing." [29]

Throughout the ages, a similar spirit animated all those who have understood the grandeur of God and who serve Him in sincerity. The builders of the Temple of Jerusalem, Christian peoples in their joy erecting our beautiful cathedrals, and the religious of every age and every country, have made this their slogan: "For God, nothing is too hard or too dear; nothing is too beautiful or too great."

In becoming complete our service confers "royalty" upon us

In popular imagination, kings are those who excel, those who surpass their competitors, peers, rivals, and enemies. In our times, "royalties" tend to multiply: there are steel kings, oil kings, movie queens, and we meet with speed kings and those of the "ring." Who will try to count the number of beauty queens who reign briefly each year?

In our turn, we dream of becoming "kings." For the love of our Master, of our Father, we are not willing to let anyone outstrip or go beyond us on the triumphal road of His service. It becomes unthinkable for us that other persons, whatever their devotion or their true heroism would do for leaders and earthly causes, could do more than we do for the King of kings and the Master of masters.

Humble religious perceive clearly to what extent their God, Whom they love so much, is far above all the rest. "I am a God without rival."

When human leaders, even the most popular, show themselves so poor, ordinarily so afflicted by limitations, faults, defects, or passions, we have the privilege of contemplating the Lord Jesus. He is the transcendent Master, the wonderful Leader, the one Who for twenty centuries has never deceived or failed His friends. He has kept His promises to them and fulfilled all their dreams, even those which seemed most fantastic.

"Kings" consecrate their kingdoms

The majesty of this Friend meditated on perseveringly always calls for the extension of our service. Newly come as we are to the first place among the multitude of those who serve, why do we not dream of consecrating and, if possible, of stabilizing the multiple activities, the innumerable actions of our "people?"

Theologians, with their learning and prudent wisdom, sometimes warn against inordinate apostolic ambitions which are often more generous and pious than efficacious. But it is still allowable for religious to rally to the wider views of St. Teresa of Avila in the matter of prayer for the Kingdom of God. We can sense that she was obsessed by the spiritual condition of continents already ravaged or threatened by heresy. One expression recurs in her writing: "a multitude of souls." [30]

Our personal activities, our works, our duties, have their human aspects; consequently they are fraternally allied with the actions of our contemporaries. We cherish the hope that our dedicated services, thus united, may take over and ennoble the sufferings of all our fellowmen. Through our offering the efforts and the work of our brothers, their research as well as their inventions, even simple and unexpected discoveries—all this could be spiritualized and exalted. And we dare to believe that, through our hands and hearts, the weariness of an entire people will rise to God as a cloud of incense. In view of the limitless variety of our complementary labors, and the love with which we can fill them, there can remain no craft, no profession, no way of life which can be remote from the consecration carried on by our lives dedicated to the service of the Father of all men.

To the glory of our religious families, it is possible and permissible to say this without fear. After the world of priests, it is in our ranks that the Lord has found the most faithful, the most loving, and the most dedicated of His servants.

"One thing I ask of the Lord, this I seek: to dwell in the house of the Lord all the days of my life, that I may gaze on the loveliness of the Lord." [31]

"His Face is my sole Fatherland." [32]

Guided by this light, all the multitude of religious are on their way to that fatherland: from contemplatives to missionaries, from teachers to hospital sisters, all serve their brethren better for having served God well. And thus it is that for fifteen centuries, humanity as a whole has profited from the beauty and "grandeur" to which we aspire with all our strength and in the sincerity of our heatrs.

III. OUR THREE VOWS

Our three vows, ever better understood and practiced, allow us at times to improve day after day the service that we give to God and to participate in all the suffering of the world in a more loving way.

The heart of man is concerned with and often possessed by three great passions—for earthly goods, for love, and for freedom. His life passes in pursuing them; his ambition as well as his obsession is to possess them in abundance.

In their filial homage to God in working to put on the perfection of Christ their model, religious struggle tirelessly to rid themselves of the last traces of these three major passions. Some religious succeed so well in purifying their hearts that they are able to moderate their ardor, and to control their thoughts, even to dry up the source of their desires and to do away with vain reveries. It is toward these heights, toward the triumphant service of so holy a God, that the most fervent religious advance and progress.

"Blessed are the clean of heart"

These hearts, disengaged, transformed, and purified, receive not only the thrilling promise of seeing for eternity the Face of God; but on this earth—and this is one of the hundredfolds promised them—they come to adopt the same viewpoints as those of God, to look at persons and things in the light that the Master of hearts casts upon them. Aloft on the heights from which they see the great ensemble, the blessed participate in the love and the compassion of God for the multitudes which follow one another in time.

Urged on by the poverty of Christ, religious are ingenious in finding ways of enlarging the part which they will take of the manifold sufferings of the truly poor.

When a religious has advanced many degrees in the Love that perfects the chaste, she gives her heart to God. The universal Father of all men utilizes it as a faithful channel. And through it, from the Heart of God Himself, there will come to the unhappy and the afflicted, the exact measure, the precise touch of tenderness and pity which in His goodness He destines for them.

Being made, in the manner and in the pattern of the Crucified One on Calvary, obedient unto death, the religious by the third vow, finishes by playing the role of companion, of instructor, and of sanctifier in the vast throng of victims of all kinds of subjections, servitudes, and of the most atrocious and most inhuman slavery.

It is good that there is permanently in the Church under the eyes of ensuing generations, a group of souls showing two things by actual experience.

1. With the grace of God, the virtues of the three vows

are lived by thousands of persons, sons and daughters of the universal Church, children of every nation.

2. It is in the exact measure in which these perfect themselves in the practice of the three vows of religion that the joy of their dedicated hearts goes forward and becomes great.

[1] Latin Patrology, LV, 165.

[2] Exodus, XXXIV, 29.

[3] Henri Bremond.

[4] Genesis, I.

[5] Daniel, III, 57.

[6] Wilson Bentley has spent more than 45 years of his life in assembling material for his great work: "Snow Crystals." He estimates that one snowfall provides at least one hundred millions of crystals, all different. The 5,300 which he shows have no similar forms.

[7] Dr. Bernard Villaret: **Fishes and Corals.**

[8] Plato: **Alcibiades.**

[9] St. Teresa of Avila, **Way of Perfection,** Ch. VII.

[10] Plato: **Ibid.**

[11] Psalms, CIII, 2.

[12] **Et sit splendor Domini Dei nostri super nos.**

[13] Ezechiel, XVI, 14. Cf. Judith, X, 4: "And the Lord increased this her beauty so that she appeared to all men's eyes incomparably lovely."

[14] Psalms, XXIII, 6.

[15] Psalms, LXXV, 4.

[16] Delcasse, French Minister of Foreign Affairs (1852-1923).

[17] Oration at Prime: **ad tuam justitiam faciendam,** etc.

[18] Contemplation on the Love of God.

[19] Quoted in **L'Ami du clergé,** 8 Nov., 1956, p. 626.

[20] St. Matthew, XI, 12.

[21] Guillore, S.J., **Les progrès de la vie spirituelle,** Paris. G. Martin, 80.

[22] Isaias, LIII, 4.

[23] Tobias, XIII, 4.

[24] Isaias, LXV, 21.

[25] Wisdom, VI, 7.

[26] Wisdom, XI, 22.

[27] Way of Perfection, Ch. XXIV.

[28] Autobiography, of St. Teresa. Translated by David Lewis. Newman Book Shop (1943) XXVI.

[29] Cf. I Chron., XXI, 24.

[30] Autobiography, Chapters XI,XXXII, XXXIV.

[31] Psalms, XXVI, 4.

[32] St. Thérèse de Lisieux, Canticle to the Holy Face, August 12, 1895.

CHAPTER II

POVERTY

Blessed are the poor in spirit for
theirs is the Kingdom of Heaven.[1]

In the very first sentence of His message given on the
Mount of the Beatitudes, Jesus declares that the possessors
of real happiness are those who are truly poor; not always
those who live in dire poverty but all those who have succeeded in making themselves poor in spirit.

Being an upright teacher, Christ lived as a really poor
man. He made clear what poverty must be if it is to be a
liberating force and a source of happiness.

The saints, who speak with authority when they comment on the thought of our Teacher, show us and teach us
what degree of detachment and self-spoliation must be
striven for by seekers of the blessedness promised to the
poor in spirit.

Having become sincerely poor, the religious of today
have a message to deliver and a mission to fulfill in the
midst of a generation whose guides and apostles they must
be. We must make the faithful understand that true poverty is that which gives us back our childhood souls. To
dwell in the Kingdom we must decrease to the size of little ones.

As true and consistent disciples of Christ, our Model

and Leader, we religious must strive to take an always larger share in the misery of the most cruelly tried of the poor—those who are hungry, those who are cold, all those who suffer in so many ways.

I. BLESSED ARE THE POOR IN SPIRIT

As a universal liberator, Jesus wishes to lessen in every man his passion to possess. Insatiable desires for lands, goods, and money have made the rich much too cruel. There have been centuries and countries in which a fortune was estimated in human beings. A single owner was sometimes the absolute master of thousands of slaves. Even today the vast majority of men, especially those who are very poor, imagine that happiness begins for a man the day that poverty is finally banished from his life and he begins to possess some money or some land. In the dreams as well as in the vocabulary of the lowly and unfortunate, the word "wealth" is habitually synonymous with "happiness." [2]

When Christ issued His great appeal, poverty, even among the Jews, was still considered a curse from God. For crowds, just as for children, nothing can take the place of the lesson taught by concrete things. In order to make His message of poverty well understood, Jesus took up His abode among the humble and the poor. Almost all men are born under a roof made by human hands; they have a lodging, however miserable, where they can settle. And it is the dream of all to die in their own home. Our Lord was born in a natural cave, the refuge of animals. Less favored than

"the foxes and the birds of the air . . . the Son of Man has nowhere to lay His head." [3]

He died finally under the open sky of His Father and on a gibbet. Thus being born, living and dying in much poorer conditions than His brethren, Christ won the right to speak to us of poverty.

The poverty that was blessed

Our Teacher has clearly given us to understand that destitution is not in itself a source and condition of happiness. What He called blessed is not a state but a spirit. Contrary to what some imagine, He did not declare all the poor blessed; neither did He curse all the rich. An unrivalled teacher, He does not judge men according to appearances, rank or condition. Having the privilege of reading hearts, He divides and classifies us according to the degree of our sincerity, desires and aspirations. If He finds free and detached souls, He makes of them His crib and His kingdom.

The proof that He has not cursed all the rich is furnished us by the Gospel. In the course of the conversation that He had with the rich young man, finding him so faithful to the decalogue and seeing his pure heart, Jesus "looked upon him and loved him." Touched by his moral excellence, Christ offered him perfection. Frightened by the despoiling proposed to him, the youth's face fell "and he went away sad, for he had great possessions."

The context of this scene allows us to add that in seeing him thus turn away forever, Jesus must have followed him with His glance and His regrets. In the apostolic college, this young man could have become the rival of St. John. When he had disappeared, the Master, sad in His turn, said to those about Him, "With what difficulty will those who trust in riches enter the kingdom of God." [4]

In spite of all, total and bitter poverty does not in itself bring a blessing. Some unfortunate people blame poverty on God and curse Him because they are poor. These are not even at the entrance of beatitude. But the shepherds at the crib, simple souls who were free from any attachment, were the very first recruits in the army of the poor, the first citizens in the Kingdom of God which is the true fatherland of souls.

Detachment from material goods

In the hope of sharing in the joy of the courtiers of this Kingdom, religious, who are especially favored by the Founder of poverty, give up their material possessions. This was the first act of their most remote predecessors. St. Anthony, the first hermit, the "Father of Monks,"

> "sold all that he possessed and distributed the price to
> the poor . . . and freed from all these obstacles, he began
> on earth a life comparable to that of the blessed." [5]

Almost a thousand years later, St. Francis of Assisi, renewing Anthony's gesture, rekindled the flame of true and holy poverty. Even in our own days, the Church, a motherly and understanding teacher, requires only one act from religious before recognizing their title of "poor." She asks them to engage themselves by vow to give up their material goods, or at least not to dispose of their revenues without the control and authorization of their superiors. Better than anyone else, the Church shares in the science of her Master. She knows how very different vocations are in the world of

souls. Some who are called never go beyond the elementary
stage. They will never take anything but the very first steps
on the long road that leads to the goal of perfect poverty;
for beyond the letter, there is a wide field with no definite
limits.

The Saints are the authorized commentators on the thought of the Master

The Church listens to the saints who comment on the
words of our Lord. In canonizing them, she consecrates their
interpretations. She invites all those who hear and understand the call of these inspired shepherds to follow their
guidance when they lead the way up to high spiritual
pastures.

St. Francis of Assisi

The passion to possess can be very compelling, but it is
not the only one that encumbers the heart of man. When
the Poor Man of Assisi launched his great appeal, vocations
came to him from all sides. Generally when a saint arises
in the Church, crowds gather around him like sheep seeking a shepherd. Among the numerous recruits that heard the
call of St. Francis were some professors who had distinguished themselves at Paris and Bologna, the most ancient
of the medieval universities. To these masters, who were
dreaming of becoming disciples again, St. Francis proposed
that they overthrow the obstacle barring their road to perfection. The professors, though possessing few worldly goods,
clung passionately to the learning of which they were so

proud. The "Poor Man" did not hesitate to ask them if they felt capable of despoiling themselves "of their knowledge as of a temporal wealth." [6] But these teachers turned away sad. The great lover of poverty seeing them withdraw, must have heard in his heart the echo of the words of Christ when He could not attach to Himself the rich young man. How difficult it is for the proud of mind to enter into the Kingdom peopled by the simple and by little ones.[7]

St. Ignatius of Loyola

The breach was made by the Poor Man of Assisi. To his epic of poverty new songs were to be added that would celebrate detachment and freedom in numerous aspects. Three and a half centuries after St. Francis of Assisi, St. Ignatius of Loyola in describing the perfection of obedience, allows us to glimpse to what lengths our poverty can be carried. Detachment and renunciation can and ought to triumph even in that domain universally recognized as the most sacred.

> It is in the sanctuary of their own heart that seekers of perfection will rally all their efforts in order to succeed in renouncing, in the most upright sincerity, their personal will and their own judgment . . .

It seems impossible to rise to such heights without a special grace, yet when one does, he discovers in superiors the "Vicars of God," the lieutenants of Christ our Lord, and

> "it is with their will and with their judgment that he will strive to frame his own."

Is not this the surest means and the most direct way to conform

> "to the first and supreme rule of judgment and will, namely, Infinite Goodness and Eternal Wisdom . . ." [8]

St. Teresa of Avila

Around 1583 traditions in regard to poverty and the manner of understanding it among the leaders of religious life were sufficiently defined so that the famous Prioress of St. Joseph's in Avila could make this fine summary of them:

> These are the arms that must be inscribed on our banners: these things we must faithfully observe in the house, in apparel, in words, and much more in our thoughts. . . . As St. Claire once said, "The walls of poverty are strong." With these united with those of humility she used to say she desired her monasteries to be enclosed.[9]

We have not progressed far enough in the knowledge of poverty as long as we have not explored the very vast domains where it can be indefinitely widened and enriched. There are heights to which sure and experienced guides can lead us and from which it is possible to contemplate a panorama revealing all the beauties and grandeurs of poverty such as it is lived in many religious families.

Renunciation and progressive impoverishment

All the riches of a human being come to him from God, but through numerous intermediaries. In a consecrated person, one can distinguish what he owes to his race, to his ancestors; then there are the qualities and the gifts that he himself has bettered, the knowledge and the culture he has gained; then again there are the skills and the authority he has acquired as well as the personality he has formed for himself. Here is a vast field which offers many opportunities for voluntary prunings. No one will dare to speak of these as mutilations when he sees the spiritual and apostolic fruits resulting from this freely chosen renunciation.

"O Brothers, if you sincerely desire to enrich yourselves,
seek eagerly for authentic wealth." [10]

The renunciation of one's personal history, past, name

In a certain community a research made by the administration revealed by chance to the religious that the humblest and most retiring of their companions was of royal blood. In that large cosmopolitan congregation, she had obtained from her major superiors, the only ones who knew of her princely origins, the permission to live far from her country in the total obscurity and heroic poverty she had won for herself. Moreover, she was rendering great service in acquitting herself perfectly of her employment.

However astonishing it may seem, local superiors may be completely ignorant of the social antecedents of some of their subjects, so discreet are these about their past. Sometimes the better to hide a distinguished personal history, they choose a religious family where they are assured of losing even their name.

Some of the faithful are surprised, even shocked, when on the day she takes the habit or makes her profession, a young religious must change her baptismal name. Their astonishment would be doubled if they knew that, in the not very distant past, a name was imposed upon her by authority without any consulting of her legitimate desires or preferences. It is sufficient to recall this reflection of an old writer:

> "All the children of the Church should have such respect for her that they would never condemn her . . . and if one does not see why she makes (or tolerates) such an ordinance, yet he would be persuaded that she does it very wisely." [11]

Up to that time a patron saint had watched over the young religious's first attempts at holiness. Far from being forgotten, he will always be loved and invoked, but another now becomes her heavenly and efficacious helper in the acquisition of all the virtues necessary in order to live well the religious life and to have a fruitful apostolate.

The anonymous in large communities

Considered from a too human viewpoint, a large community may seem a cavern where all are on a deadly level. How indeed in a group of religious at prayer can one distinguish the professor of philosophy from the sister cook? One may know that, lost and mingled with the others, there is one who came out a brilliant first in a competition with hundreds of other nurses. One could discover those who have a master's degree, even a doctorate. Others for many years have had hundreds of their pupils successful in difficult examinations. Identical veils and habits make all uniform.

In their meditations, these sisters say to themselves that

God is not concerned about our distinctions; He does not conform to our measuring rods. "Our grandeurs make Him smile."

Among these persons only one rivalry seems desirable— the winning of the riches with which God adorns the soul.

Sisterly equality in death

By degrees as their earthly existence wears away, religious within the humble enclosure of the motherhouse, are brought, one after another, to the community cemetery. It is there that all the distinctions and divisions that may have existed end by being effaced. How, in the shadow of the crosses that are all alike, can one distinguish the learned from the ignorant, those of high social origin from the humble daughters of the poor? Who will succeed in identifying those born among old Christian nations or those who, though born in paganism, ended their lives in the fullness of sanctity?

Some ten or fifteen years later, another sister will be buried by the side of one of her predecessors. Rain will efface the names on the crosses. These will be found in the community archives, but how, after many years, can one distinguish a certain sister among the hundreds of Sisters Mary, Joseph, Peter, Paul? And Sisters Luke, Augustine, Ambrose, Dominic, Thomas, Ignatius, Theresa, are too numerous for one to identify with certainty a religious who has lovingly given forty or fifty years of her life to the service of Christ and His brethren. Long before the recent campaigns for just one class of marriage and burial, the old tradition of our Mother, the Church, was perpetuated among us, teaching us the great brotherhood of Christians in the face of death.

An archeologist, after exploring the subterranean tombs

in the region of Sousse in Tunisia, wrote in the beginning of the twentieth century:

> The catacombs show the spirit of true equality, of true fraternity, that reigned among the first Christians. See these "loculi" which are all the same, except for two or three (doubtless the tombs of bishops) out of fifteen thousand and more . . . without distinction of origin or class; the faithful, rich and poor, great and lowly, rest side by side. . . . These galleries form as it were a single tomb, a real family tomb. . . . Even in death, one can say of the first Christians, "See how they loved one another." [12]

II. POVERTY TRANSFORMS SOULS

Among its numerous advantages, poverty sincerely lived gives us a twofold wealth:

> It frees us from the limitations and the prejudices that tyrannize over many of our brethren.

> It gives us again the soul of a child.

Freedom through poverty

The uniformity described above, which may seem frightful to some, is in fact the condition of emancipation.

We do not extinguish our talents nor render them sterile, but we no longer glory in them. We develop them through charity; we cultivate them in simplicity. We make our sisters the first to profit from them. In the world of souls, hierarchies are built only on spiritual values. Study and learning become a service, just as much as hospitality and manual work. Culture becomes a means of glorifying God and aiding our brethren. With these perspectives, we escape ridiculous pride and so-called superiority which too often separate one from those about her, intimidate and keep away the humble, the ignorant, the great crowds of those who are afflicted by their poverty and humiliated by their limitations.

"Charity is not pretentious, not puffed up." [13]

We have made the blessed discovery of a learning that does not inflate us but makes us more sisterly by the insight it gives and the pity that it increases a hundredfold.

A persevering ascesis prepares the personality of apostles

Knowing how impatience, rudeness, and lack of adaptation exasperate aching hearts, religious devote themselves to a persevering ascesis. Thus they become progressively more serene and more gentle. At times with heroism, they have impoverished themselves, freed themselves of their preferences and personal tastes. Some succeed—not without enduring efforts—in triumphing over the spontaneity of their reflexes and the natural vivacity of their answers. They have learned that all that may humiliate and drive away the poor who are to be evangelized.

This is the fruit of those secret victories, those ceaselessly wider conquests that these apostles, living images of the sweetness of God, offer in the service of the poor of Jesus Christ.

Towards this goal thousands of religious advance in a

friendly rivalry. A good number reach it. It is then that they benefit from the hundredfold promised by our God, so prodigal of His wealth. The assurance given by Christ [14] can be extended indefinitely. The hundredfold found in relatives and lands is only an encouraging symbol. One of the great laws of the Gospel is: every renunciation, every voluntary impoverishment confer spiritually the right to gains and profits of all kinds. Even on the purely human plane, it is a rare and enviable achievement for one to free himself, in the face of brilliant success, from every trace of vanity, of disdain, and above all of contempt for the too numerous victims of failure.

There are results that are scarcely believable, but it is impossible to doubt them after having so often encountered them in so many souls in every country. Having freed themselves from multiple tyrants, these souls have succeeded— not without wrenches and blows—in making their hearts so "poor" that regrets are silenced and desires end by being extinguished.

Poverty gives us back the soul of a child

Having climbed these heights, we have the impression of having forced and passed through the narrow door of the Kingdom. An indescribable happiness awaits us. Texts, the sayings of God, which we have up to now admired as it were from the outside, are at last lived. We thank the Divine Promiser for having kept His agreements in a measure beyond all our hopes.

We can repeat on our own account the letter the Machabees sent to the inhabitants of Sparta:

We have no longer need of allies and friends, having for
our comfort the holy books that are in our hands.[15]

How good God is to the upright; the Lord to those who
are clean of heart.[16]

Two certainties make our peace unshakable and increase
our hope. God is fidelity itself. What He has done for our
predecessors He will do again for our advantage. The affinity
that links religious souls to one another through the centuries,
provides us with intuitions and divinations that aid us to
understand past successes. It is then with a touching approxi-
mation that we discover the mentality and the spirit of our
guides on the road of freedom-giving poverty. We believe
with all our might that the religious who were Doctors of
the Church, founders of new schools of spirituality, authentic
scholars, and great superiors, all kept a child-like soul. In
the intimate life of their community, St. Thomas Aquinas
and St. Bonaventure were extremely simple religious; so
also were St. Ignatius of Loyola, St. John of the Cross, St.
Teresa of Avila and St. Therese of Lisieux. Superiors could
pay homage to the total simplicity of the celebrated Mabil-
lon; of Mendel, the Austrian Augustinian; and the Italian
Jesuit Secchi. Even when they could foresee the fame that
would be attached one day to their names, and even if God
would have shown them in advance the crowds whose guides
and teachers they would become in the courses of ages, it
is impossible for us to doubt that they succeeded in having
"hearts virgin of all human glory." [17]

Our generation has known religious who have attained
celebrity. The daily witnesses of their unrelenting work, the
superiors who have governed them and who received their

filial confidences, do not hesitate to proclaim that they were the simplest and the most docile members of their community; the most obliging also, being generous almsgivers of their vast erudition and taking their share with others in the commonest material work.

It is usual to meet in communities of women, great superiors who, after having brilliantly directed their religious family, have re-entered the ranks often with delightful simplicity. They obey with evident joy the younger sisters whose venerated mistresses they had been in the novitiate. To hundreds of disciples these guides taught and revealed the beauties and grandeurs of religious life. Today their theories are cofirmed by the irreplaceable eloquence of example. Their indisputable accomplishments and their continued success did not take from them their child-like souls.

Little ones are ignorant of many things; there is one thing of which they do not know even the name, still less the meaning. This is *glory*. It is told that the governor of a king who was still very young displayed his total lack of psychology. His pedagogical sense was even poorer. To the small Louis XV he showed with pomposity palaces and crowds, saying, "Sire, all this belongs to you." [18] The child opened his eyes wide, but it was evident that he understood nothing of this speech.

Happy are the adults who have understood for all time that God alone is great. They are set in a simplicity that makes them approachable, indulgent, kind. They have taken a place and a rank in that court where the favorites of the King are the humble, the little ones and all those who have decreased to the stature of these privileged beings.[19]

III. PARTICIPATION IN THE SUFFERINGS OF THE POOR

"O God, Thou art the Father of little ones, the recourse
of the persecuted, the strength of the weak, the refuge
of the humble, the redeemer of those who have no other
hope." [20]

In the hearts of thousands of religious great love of God
is united to love of the poor. Impelled alternately by these
two forces, those who are eager to understand, love, and give
themselves, become capable of every kind of compassion
and sisterly assimilation. These favorites of the Father of
all men are obsessed by a fact and a figure. Humanity today
will soon number three thousand millions of human beings.
Of these masses, two-thirds are poor, never having enough
to satisfy their hunger. The friends of God feel and understand that He wishes to have His "share" in this immense
and permanent suffering measured out to the earth and to
races. For this purpose God utilizes the bodies of the best
of His children, the men and women who have consecrated
themselves to His exclusive and total service. Vocations will
be awakened, and they will differ from one another according to the tone of the call and the attraction felt for certain
types of self-immolation. The infinite goodness of God has
made our hearts varied enough that He can make them share
in all the phases of His pity. Not a single form of poverty will
be forgotten or neglected.

God Who loves every individual in the great crowds of
the poor will have each one's share of affection reach him
through the messenger chosen for this mission. We are
sorry that we are not numerous enough to bring to every

one the fitting and fatherly help destined for him by our Father in Heaven.

The Aid Given by the Penitential Orders

There is one kind of help that is full of mystery and whose mode of application we do not grasp. It certainly reaches all the victims of poverty. This is the aid always given them by the religious of the Penitential Orders. The aims of these men and women are diverse and their conceptions complementary. Some consecrated persons pray, fast, and mortify themselves in every way in order to compensate for the immense amount of praise of which God is deprived. He is too poorly known to be served and loved. Reparation and the praise of compensation are traditional among contemplatives.

Other generous souls give themselves to a penitential order because they have the assurance of finding in it a means of sharing in their own flesh the sufferings of the poor. These privileged souls understand by a light which never leads astray that Christ's pity was not monopolized, still less exhausted, by the crowds He met in Palestine. There He found the unfortunate, the hungry, the leprous, the blind, the paralytic; there also were the victims of every form of unkindness, those overwhelmed by humiliations, disdain, and contempt. Now this mass of miseries is transmitted; it is the inevitable heritage of the human race. Poverty comes down through all the centuries; it passes over all obstacles and like death, it mocks at our frontiers.

Among the multiple aspects of their magnificent vocation, the penitents know that it is for them, more than for others, to maintain in the Church that "extra humanity," [21] which, utilized by the loving Christ, permits Him to take

His personal share in the least of the sufferings endured by the most insignificant of the children of men.

Great spiritual facts would give strength and enthusiasm if they could become palpable and visible. For some the mystery of our cloisters would be clarified in this way. Our broadcasting stations and relays for television are often placed in a flat counrtyside or on isolated hills. At night red lights indicate their antennae. Here is a modernized symbol of our Carthusian, Cistercian, Carmelite, and Poor Clare monasteries. The crowds have only a confused idea of the role of broadcasting towers, but even stranger to them are the monastic buildings, whether vast or modest, which are sometimes surrounded by high walls like prisons or penitentiaries.

We forget that beyond the noise of radio apparatus peddling news, speeches, appeals, operas or songs, there are waves of another order circulating through another world. The souls of the children of the same Father know and feel that they are brethren. Without seeing or knowing one another, they meet in the marvelous country of love, pity, and compassion.

All religious have to participate in
the multiple sufferings of the poor

At every hour of the day and night, poor people are hungry. Others suffer from cold or are tortured in their bodies. To all this are added disappointments, failures, humiliations. Poverty with its hundred faces is always visiting the world of the afflicted. God asks all of us to make ourselves the auxiliaries and the aids of His pity.

"I was hungry . . ."[22]

The monastic fast has partly for its aim to imitate and honor the hunger of the poor. The starving, exasperated by their painful suffering, cry out against the inefficaciousness of this kind of pity. Though it is delayed, the meal of voluntary fasters is finally served to them. In His foreseeing love, the Lord, attentive to every distress, carefully wards off this reproach, which is indeed excusable because it is caused by an excess of suffering. In the Church are to be found religious women (and I have met some of them) who suffer habitually from hunger. Their importance and place God alone knows, but together with the too large number of Christians suffering from hunger, this group permits Christ to say in this generation as in all preceding ones, "I was hungry with you and like you. . . ."

"I was naked . . ."[23]

Therefore exposed to cold and heat. According to seasons and latitudes, religious today actualize this complaint of the Lord Who is always living in His poor. Their enormous monasteries or humble convents are, in many cases, not heated, still less air-conditioned. One is morally sure that it will be thus for a long time, perhaps forever. It is a promise of Christ that will not pass away: "The poor you have always with you." [24] If, as certain ones hope, we shall succeed in banishing poverty from the earth, it will be for poor religious to open the doors of their homes to this "exile."

Our imagination, however powerful, will succeed only imperfectly in realizing what a Trappist or Carmelite monastery must be like in the course of winters that are particularly cold and humid. Novices discover this experimentally during their year of trial. Then it is with complete liberty they choose this atmosphere for all the winters of their life. As these interminable months roll by, these sincere friends of the poor improve their knowledge of what cold is. After twenty or thirty years, they know all its aspects.

During prayers, thanksgivings, or office chanted in an icy chapel or in one where the walls sweat with dampness, they have won the right and the privilege of joining mystically the old and the children who suffer enough to weep on account of the cold that benumbs them or the humidity that penetrates them. These religious know how to compassionate the distress of mothers who are powerless to dry the tears of their shivering children or to protect them from the cough that racks them. They receive in their flesh and in their hearts all these widely-spread sufferings. They clothe these miseries with their own pains and offer all to God, making use of the compassionate words of Scripture: "Happy is he who has regard for the lowly and the poor." [25]

It is as if in the great silence of snow-covered countries, through gusts of wind or the downpour of rain, beneficial waves circulate, bringing both the suffering that calls for pity and the answering love that consecrated souls pour forth on their friends, the poor.

In the course of torrid summers, the poor suffer in their miserable attics under a burning roof or in improvised shelters in the shanty towns throughout the world. Some religious missionaries pass their lives in the exhausting heat of the tropics, and these other aspects of the misery of the poor cannot find them or leave them indifferent. How many religious women have their cells under roofs of zinc, slate, or tile! After days of laborious work, they experience stifling nights which make sleep difficult and sometimes impossible. All this unites them fraternally to the poor.

"Relatives" of the poor

Having the same lot and sharing the same suffering are not sufficient for hearts that love the poor. Numerous religious families contract different kinds of relationships with the needy (their names, popular in all countries, bear witness to this). Everybody knows the Little Sisters of the Poor and the Daughters of Charity. Some religious do not hesitate to proclaim that the poor are their masters; they claim only one title—that of the Servants of the Poor.

We do not sufficiently realize to what extent these names are lived in all sincerity. When the love of Christ, the great friend of the poor, invades the heart of a simple and upright religious, when she has given herself once for all to a love without respite, her human existence is consumed like a candle. Hurried visitors, whose feelings lack depth, believe that they should pity sisters who pass their lives in some small country hospice where harassed administrators have assembled and packed together the incurables, the idiots, and the misfits of a whole region. We can guess what the occupations of these Servants of the Poor must be. They quickly learn to love their charges whom they contemplate with the eyes of God.

In every human being, whoever he may be, and in spite of his weaknesses, defects, his sordid poverty, even in spite of his repulsive vices, a holy religious soon finds beneath all these veils the faithful image of her Master. After Holy Communion, some Hospital Sisters recite this prayer before returning to their tasks,

"O my adorable Savior, it is You Whom I have the honor
of serving in the person of the poor." [26]

The most wretched of their children are transfigured. In
their service, as in the service of God Himself, nothing
appears too hard or too difficult. Natural pride, reputation,
and what in human language is called dignity, all this will
be sacrificed and immolated as in the fire of a holocaust.
Before we had our modern organizations and social agencies,
the religious of all countries knew how to spare the poor
that gesture which some of them find the most humiliating,
that of holding out their hand to beg. Rich persons, who
voluntarily had become poor, went from door to door, expos-
ing themselves to insults, contemptuous refusals, cutting and
ironical remarks. Their delicate sensitiveness might be tortured, but they considered that they were not paying too
high a price for the joy of seeing their masters, their "lords,"
the poor, freed from the humiliation of exhibiting their distress, of revealing to all that they were hungry.

When one has felt and shared, even mystically experienced, the goodness of God towards the poor, one knows
how much He wishes them to be treated with extreme tact
and delicacy. This is revealed only to the disciples that are
deeply versed in the science of poverty. Such a science exists,
even though there is no academy in the world that teaches
it. Like all other sciences, that of poverty has its laws. These
teach us that there are never two poor persons who live out
their trial in an identical way. Each type of poverty consti-
tutes a unique world, and the friends of the poor eagerly
draw near every one of these that our kind Lord asks them
to explore in turn. Every new exploration profits by the
knowledge gleaned from the hundreds of the poor already

helped. The day finally comes when one's memory and heart possess a living doctrine fragrant with love and much more valuable and fruitful than the best organized filing cabinets.

Possessing this real spiritual wealth and having a spirit that is never lost once it is well assimilated, religious can plunge into the crowds of unfortunates that are awaiting them. The science they have acquired insures them from ever humiliating anyone and allows them to adapt themselves to the complexity as well as to the tragedy of the saddest cases. Those called to this mission can say:

"Thanks be to God Who always leads us in triumph in Christ Jesus, manifesting through us the odor of His knowledge in every place. For we are the fragrance of Christ." [27]

[1] St. Matthew, V, 3.

[2] A mosaic at Pompeii declares, **Lucrum est gaudium.** True happiness is to get rich.

[3] St. Luke, IX, 58.

[4] St. Mark, X, 17-21.

[5] Breviary, January 17, Lesson IV.

[6] **Dictionary of Catholic Theology.** "The Friars Minor."

[7] St. Matthew, XI, 25, and XVIII, 3.

[8] **Constitutions of the Society of Jesus,** Part III, Chapter I, 23.

[9] **The Way of Perfection.**

[10] Sexagesima Sunday, Anthem of None.

[11] Quoted by Henri Bremond in his **Histoire litteraire,** Vol. IX, p. 175.

[12] Mgr. Leynaud: **Les Catacombes africaines,** 2nd edition, 1922. Carbonel, Algiers.

[13] I Corinthians, XIII, 4.

[14] St. Mark, X, 29, 31.

[15] I Machabees, XII, 9.

[16] Psalms, LXII, 1.

[17] Henri Bremond, op. cit., VII, 100.

[18] Marichal Francois de Villeroi (1644-1730).

[19] St. Augustine's commentary on Psalm 118, "What is a child? Humility personified."

[20] Adapted from the prayer of Judith.

[21] Colossians, I, 24. Cf. Sister Elizabeth of the Trinity.

[22] St. Matthew, XXV, 35.

[23] Ibid., 36.

[24] St. Mark, XIV, 7.

[25] Psalms, XL, 2.

[26] Morning Prayer of the Hospital Sisters of St. Thomas of Villeneuve.

[27] II Corinthians, II, 14-15.

CHAPTER III

CHASTITY

> "The unmarried woman thinks about the things of the Lord, that she may be holy in body and spirit." [1]

It is not easy for us to arrange the beauties and grandeurs of our religious lives in an absolutely sure hierarchy of values, but we have, however, the feeling that chastity raises us towards the heights. We cannot enumerate all the advantages that it brings to us. However, we shall say how much it increases our love, how much it instills in religious the secret and the strength of a dedication more complete and more lasting than that of mothers. In accord with all human hearts, our own as well as all others wish for wonderful affections. Chastity assures us even on this earth of a magnificent compensation, the hundredfold of all the human loves we have sacrificed.

The age-old dream, but one always doomed to disappointment, is to discover the way leading to a great and ever-increasing love and to make it eternal. This foolish hope becomes for us a reality because it is given to us to love God, Christ, and the Virgin Mother. In demanding of consecrated persons all the love of their hearts, God does not blunt nor destroy our power of loving. He increases it a hundredfold. The great Friend of little ones and of the weak does not take out of the hearts of women their maternal instinct. He makes it "divine" and carries it to the height of greatness and sublimity. God has made and still makes religious more heroically devoted than mothers according to the flesh. There are, then, two ways in which chastity confers royalty: it multiplies love and makes it universal. It permits sometimes that certain religious "reign" over the world of mothers.

I. CHASTITY INCREASES OUR LOVE

The Holy Trinity, in the Person of the Father, said one day to St. Teresa of Avila:

> "The gifts and graces which I have heaped upon you are My own Son, the Holy Spirit, and the Blessed Virgin. What can you offer to Me to prove to Me your gratitude?" [2]

These words God repeats to all consecrated souls. Infinite Tenderness describes the marvelous world of our Loves, and makes known to us the impressive names of our Friends. Beyond all the poor loves which move our brothers to passion and with which they have to be content, we are invited to love the Infinite Love, Jesus Christ, and the sweet Virgin Mary.

1. The Love of God

"God is love," [3] therefore the inexhaustible source and the boundless ocean of it. The most beautiful and the most heroic loves, and the most disinterested gifts of self are only poor crumbs fallen from the table of the eternal feast. And it is to this eternal banquet that God invites us. In order to try to teach us what is the "breadth and length and height and depth" [4] of His love, the Divine Teacher invites us to listen to inspired authors who have heaped up comparisons. The love of God, being infinite, is at the same time more tender than that of mothers, more "passionate" than that of lovers, but above all its almighty power helps us to make magnificent realities of our foolish dreams. As to its fidelity, it is far beyond and above that of lovers and that of friends.

God loves us as does a mother

God loves us through the heart of our mothers and it is in starting from and tracing back these consoling experiences that it is possible for us to explore or to glimpse some aspects of the tenderness of God. In the evening of their lives how many human beings recall the story of their loves, admitting that they have never been more or better loved than by their own mothers!

The love that God bears us commences with our very life. It precedes that of our mothers.

"You have been my guide since I was first formed, my security at my mother's breast. From my mother's womb, you are my God." [5]

If parents reject the fruit of their love, God offers Himself as a Father to orphans:

"Though my father and mother forsake me, yet the Lord will receive me." [6]

The source which feeds and keeps ever fresh the tenderness of our mothers pours forth into us permanently the most delightful of loves:

> "The Most High will be more tender to you than a mother." [7]

> "You shall be carried at the breasts . . . and they shall caress you.

> "As one whom the mother caresseth, so will I comfort you." [8]

Invisible, but very loving, God watches over our cradles. A contemplative one day had the comparison forcibly impressed on her. God seemed to murmur to her,

> "I have for you all the vigilance and the devotion that a doctor has for his own children."

*God's love is stronger and more tender
than the love of lovers or of spouses*

Parallels can be made. Human loves, no matter how satisfactory, cannot be anything but transitory. Their completeness is only intermittent. Addressing Himself to a human soul, the Creator said:

> "And I will espouse thee to Me in faith and thou shalt know that I am the Lord." [9]

We are not ignorant of the lyricism to which lovers abandon themselves. They remain always powerless to realize their most daring and most foolish dreams. The Creator gives us, His cherished children, the right to speak to Him in words like these:

"Where can I go from Your spirit?
From Your Presence, where can I flee?
If I go up to the heavens, You are there;
If I sink to the nether world, You are present there;
If I take the wings of the dawn,
If I settle at the farthest limits of the sea,
Even there Your hand shall guide me
And Your right hand shall hold me fast." [10]

With such a God, all loving souls have their part in these intimacies which He allows those greatly privileged:

"The Lord used to speak to Moses face to face, as one friend speaks to another." [11]

"And David went on growing and increasing, and the Lord of hosts was with him." [12]

Fidelity of God in His Love

What compared to ours can the *Always* of lovers mean to us? The Master of the universe offers us sublime images for the permanence of His love.

"May His Name be praised forever:
As long as the sun, His Name shall remain." [13]

"Of old You established the earth, and the heavens
are the work of Your hands. They shall perish, but You
remain though all of them grow old like a garment. . . .
But You are the same and Your years have no end." [14]

The promises of our Divine Friend are explicit and consoling beyond measure:

"Until the evening of your lives, you will find Me faithful; when your hair shall grow white, My strength and
my arms will be your support." [15]

It is with the certainty of being heard that the friends
of God murmur as they near the end of their days:

"Now that I am old and gray, O God, do not forsake me.
My strength has forsaken me; remain with me in Thy
fidelity. . . . I am bent with age, weighed down with
years, O remain my companion." [16]

With enthusiasm the dialogue proceeds throughout the
Holy Scriptures:

"For the mountains shall be moved and the hills shall
tremble; but My mercy shall not depart from thee and
the covenant of My peace shall not be moved." [17]

Such is the beautiful story of our love on earth, but it is
still only a shining symbol of the eternal love with which the
unchanging youth of God will enrapture us:

"I know that I shall dwell in the house of the Lord for
years to come." [18]

The Love of God makes us like to Him

All love is assimilating, that of God much more so than that of others. When the soul has found this love, it begins to love in a way which is liberal and universal:

"The compassion of man is toward his neighbor: but the mercy of God is upon all flesh." [19]

As all is royal in our lives, so our love also is royal. It is the King Who loves us and He teaches us to love the multitude. With the exception of priests, sisters are among the persons who have loved the great masses of humanity more and better than others. The unique and ever-developing love which they bear to God comes back in deeds of charity to people created and loved by the Father of all. In order to stimulate our love, this great Friend, the incomparable Teacher, offers us two models—our Lord Jesus Christ and His Virgin Mother.

2. The Love of Christ

With individual variations which only Infinite Love can create, the history of the love that religious have for Christ and the dilection which they receive through it can bring about an enviable harmony.

They have left the world because God has come into their lives. Until then they had not loved Him more nor less than others. One day He drew so near that they could hear the murmur of His call, "Come, follow Me." [20]

In order to follow Him, they have suffered heart rending renunciations or heroic separations. It has been necessary for them to tear themselves from the embrace of a dearly loved mother. How many of them, amid tears, leave younger brothers and sisters whom, as eldest, they have loved and to whom they have been so completely devoted. They offer up these wonderful human affections. Some postulants in a tempting prospect, have caught a glimpse of the family of which they could have become the friend and the happy mother.

It is necessary to bury themselves in a life that a great number (even among Christians) think to be inhuman and intolerable; to become poor and dependent to the point of having nothing to dispose of without permission; to dream of being chaste when imperious appeals to their passions clamor in them; to sacrifice definitely and totally that which is more personal and more dear: their liberty.

This is the common lot of all those who consecrate themselves to God by the three Vows of religion. But Christ is their Master, a Master Who we know has over us only rights. He can, then, demand from us other testimonies of fidelity and love. Some religious have discovered the measure of their attachment, the transcendence of their love for Christ, on the day when they set out for exile, banished from their dearly loved country. Others, for years without Sacraments, in quarries, in mines, in prisons, or in concentration camps, persevere in giving to their only Friend the most heroic testimony. With the grace of their Master, religious of all countries hope that they will have the strength to rise towards the heights of an heroically faithful love. All hope that whatever happens, they would be incapable of betraying or denying this Friend. In unforgettable moments such marvelous fidelity is often prepared. Christ becomes known gradually, especially in the Holy Eucharist, which is the great purveyor of sanctity in the Church. At long intervals one is, as it were, aware of the mysterious presence of the Friend. There are single instants in which one is carried far away to the country of delights, breathing in that love which must be experienced before it can be comprehended. It is that divine peace of which the Apostle speaks

"which surpasses all understanding. (May it) guard your hearts and mind in Christ Jesus." [21]

In ineffable and ever-increasing exchanges, we assimilate, day after day, some elements of the immense love of our Savior for mankind. In the sincere and pledged hearts of religious there is nourished and renewed a dedication which nothing can destroy. There, new perceptions alert and refine intuitions and instincts which are so precious to those who console others.

Each morning their Master inspires religious throughout the world with the words, actions, and skillful devices by which the sick, the afflicted, and even the despairing will profit. When their hearts have been prepared by all the despoilments of exacting and logical poverty, the Friend of the little ones and the humble pours into them the abundant and transforming love which He destines for the poor, the misunderstood, the humiliated, and the poorly loved. At the end of their thanksgivings, the religious disperse, and submerge themselves in the sea of human woe, attentive and understanding dispensers of the mercy of Christ.

This Master is a leader in the ways of love. Saint Teresa of Avila, who had so deeply studied and known Him, has the right to speak to consecrated souls with authority and weight. She tells us that it is in the exact measure in which we find and know this Friend well that He makes it possible to give ourselves to still greater apostolates:

> "Since here in this life, when a person is married, she first knows with whom she is to live and who her husband is, and what he has; shall not *we* who are already contracted, think on our Spouse before the nuptials? . . . Since then those who are espoused in the world are allowed to have such thoughts, (should we) not know who this person is, and who is his father, and what kind of country that is to which he is to conduct us, or what those good things are which he promises to give us, what his good qualities are, how we may best please him and in what we can delight him, and to study how to make our will bend to his?" [22]

"Possessed" and carried away by the love which they have for God, religious souls

> "are ready to do all for the good of the neighbor. They would give their lives thousands of times to assure their brethren the smallest spiritual good. Oh! how truly extraordinary is this need to love! Our ideal as well as our purpose is to conform ourselves to the prince of love, Jesus, our all!" [23]

It is because Jesus is so much and so well loved by the chaste that the most unhappy as well as the most afflicted of the human family see coming toward them good Cyrenians, who aid them to carry their intolerably heavy crosses.

3. The Love of the Most Holy Virgin

It is only in heaven that many of the saved will understand the sanctity drawn by the multitude of religious from the sincere and filial love they bore to Mary, their Mother.

Two expressions uttered by the Blessed Virgin have lifted thousands of religious lives to the heights of heroism:

"Behold the handmaid of the Lord." [24]
"Do whatever He tells you." [25]

"Behold the handmaid of the Lord"

From the manger to the sepulchre, Mary remained faithful to this first saying. It is through having contemplated and understood the example of their model that so many consecrated souls have served their Master with acts of fidelity and with attentions of which He is truly the Only One to Whom their number and secrecy is known. From contemplatives to religious nurses, from teachers to missionaries, they devise daily new forms of devotedness. The constant contemplation of the faithful Virgin gradually makes them like that universal Mother, whose titles, the Church in her litanies never exhausts: Health of the weak, Consoler of the afflicted, Refuge of sinners, Help of Christians. . . .

Religious try to become the living replicas of our Lady of Mercy. St. Bernadette, a faithful and studious disciple of our Lady, noticing some young couples in the great public park nearby Saint Gildard de Nevers, remarked: "How much those are to be pitied who are not chaste." Chastity acquired and well understood in the visions of Massabielle had made her understanding and compassionate to all forms of human frailty. It is on account of having acquired this absolute devotion in the school of the Virgin Mother, that many religious of all countries can humbly take as their own the assurances of St. Paul to the faithful at Thessalonica:

"We in our love for you would gladly have imparted to you not only the Gospel of God, but also our own dear souls, because you had become most dear to us." [26]

"Do whatever He tells you"

One of the oldest universities of Europe, that of Oxford, keeps its proud motto, "Deus illuminatio mea" [27] "The Lord is my light." The words of the Gospel are the source of efficacious knowledge. "Do whatever He tells you." This simple advice of the Mother of Jesus has illumined and transformed existences by the thousands. Humble religious, sometimes without much formal education, have made prodigious discoveries in the domain of charity. No disease or affliction remains without help. All charitable foundations are the echo of the simple suggestion made to Jesus by His Mother.

Immense motherhouses where religious live and are formed are the monumental projections of this maternal counsel of the Virgin to souls anxious to carry out the desires of their Master. Sublime words, comforting or enlightening, heroic actions, unlimited devotion throughout the world, are the fruit of silent thanksgivings, in which they seem to hear the words: "Do whatever He tells you." All nations (or almost all!) have received their apostles. Not a member of the immense family of the Universal Father can be neglected or forgotten: "Do whatever He tells you." One can be convinced that from the far-away origin of religious life the maternal advice of the Virgin has been constantly followed. Unpublicized ingenuity in the giving of self, delicate attentions, innumerable acts witnessed only by God and by the happy beneficiaries—children, the poor, the humble, and the afflicted—have or will become the efficacious echoes of that recommendation made to the waiters at Cana by the Mother of Jesus: "Do whatever He tells you." The Mother of Fair Love remains the model and the animating spirit of the unwearying gift of the great world of the chaste.

II. THE FRUITFULNESS OF CHASTITY

1. Chastity increases love a hundredfold

By the vow of chastity, young religious consecrate to God all their powers of loving. To this total gift, the Sovereign Master will answer as He alone knows how to do. In hearts so fitted to become maternal, the Heavenly Father sends down floods of His love. A veritable spiritual and apostolic epic begins. All nations of the world have their crowds of children or old people, of sick or wounded, of afflicted and deformed. These young apostles will become their most loving mothers. It is these forms of anticipated maternity which they celebrate with calm or triumphant joy on the morning of profession.

Contemplatives

To those dedicated to chanting His praise God gives the honor and happiness of unlimited spiritual maternity. During the long hours passed before the Tabernacle or the

Monstrance, their dreams become clear. Some visions are concerned with unhappy multitudes among which the adorers recognize a great company of fellowmen. In it wander aimlessly refugees, exiles, displaced persons, and expatriates, many too wretched to be taken in by countries which reject them. Again they can see in this lamentable crowd children without parents and mothers without children, the mutilated, and the victims of all sorts of barbarities. This is a great starved multitude, still more eager for mercy and love than for bread or rice. A religious in prayer knows and feels by another form of knowledge than that of the economist these immeasurable distresses.

In the presence of the Savior and the Friend of men, she receives even on this earth the hundredfold for voluntary chastity. She, the spouse of Christ, from one Communion to another, becomes a sort of "universal mother." Her love, aligning itself and modeling itself on that of the Divine Friend, pours out on sorrowful humanity.

She knows that all her sisters, the visitors of the poor, the sick, the troubled, the distressed, or the humiliated, are being sustained by her incessant supplications. Does she not have the advantage of living near the ever-fresh source of the infinite mercy of God? The love of other mothers is given out and exhausts itself in their beautiful mission to the advantage of their homes. That of "universal mothers" sees itself offered throughout the expanse of a world.

Teachers

In Chapter X, St. Mark tells us that among the hundredfolds promised by Christ to those who leave all to follow Him, there is a hundredfold of "children" found with the rest.

Religious teachers in gratitude and joy receive a solid and unquestionable testimony of this. Like the majority of religious women, they have made the heroic sacrifice of renouncing forever the ineffable happiness of having children of their own flesh. God Who asks this of them knows how to appreciate this holocaust better than anyone else. He likewise is in a position to recompense them far beyond all their expectations and their hopes. The virginity of their love has opened in their hearts an inexhaustible spring of maternal tenderness. In the inspiring inventory of their desires, teachers or guardians of children discover with amazement the majestic power of these attractions. They feel that the need of dedication, "the violence" of the desires [29] which rise in their hearts will never be satisfied by exclusive service to ten or fifteen children. Each year thirty children come to quench their thirst at the ever-renewed waters of their generous love. The next year thirty others come to take the places of those who leave. Sometimes forty or fifty years passed in the orphanages or in schools will leave educators and these real mothers with the fresh tenderness of their early days. God, the Promiser of the time of their profession, will never fail to keep up and to renew their youth with that fidelity and that constancy which He employs in renewing the springtime of the year.

From the dawn of her consecrated life, a virgin has obtained from the Heart of God a maternal knowledge sometimes superior to that of mothers of even the largest families. It is a new hundredfold for those who are so generally forgotten on "Mother's Day." Maternal affections are always unique because they have to be adapted to children who are entirely different. Five or twenty times, if it is necessary, a mother will begin again with each of her children a history of which she alone knows all the secrets. Inspired and guided by the science of God, the maternal affection of a religious will almost always succeed in adapting itself to hundreds of children who will, in turn, people the primary classes or the higher groups. These divine hundredfolds bud forth in many different ways. Teaching Sisters, intimates of the great Friend of youth, will discover ways to bring together and to make real the greatest varieties of affection. Illuminated and guided by the science of their Master, religious will receive from Him a sure instinct which will eliminate psychological errors injurious to the young love which is awakened.

The Christian educator feels that she should not have the same love for a child provided with love through its mother whom it sees each night, and for the unfortunate child who has never been loved or has been inadequately loved. And it is still a new love which she makes a point of giving to the orphans who never knew the mother who died in giving them birth.

Religious teachers and educators give out and renew their love as well as their maternal comprehension in dealing with many young people. Their pupils will remember all their lives the feeling of having been truly loved by these mothers, faithful and docile instruments of the goodness of the Heavenly Father. These formations are schools in themselves. In being well loved one learns how to love, and one discovers the splendor of love.

In all the parishes of the world, youthful homes are multiplied, solid hopes of long lines of Christians, and thousands of families experience the profound joys of beautiful human loves. Often in our schools and boarding schools we can find the unknown and disinterested artisans of these various forms of happiness. At the end of the Nuptial Mass, the priest addresses the young couple thus:

"May the God of Abraham, of Isaac, and of Jacob be with you. May He fulfill His promise in you that you may see your children's children even to the third and forth generation."

The religious educators know and believe that their spiritual posterity will go on increasing without measure and propagating itself in time. The ideal they have awakened in hearts will never die. Many years after their departure from the earth, it will still influence lives and families.

The Nursing Sisters

Through her love a mother becomes capable of unlimited devotion. It is normal that God in taking possession of the heart of a religious nurse should offer for this generous gift in some cases the power of going beyond even maternal love. Thus she may become capable of taking the place of mothers in heroism, surpassing their perseverance and their courage. There are those who take the place of the mother at the side of the prodigal, the hunted, and the wretched; or with prisoners whose mothers never follow them in the jails.

2. Far beyond the love of mothers

In the service of the abnormal

It is a terrible trial for a mother to have in her family of children an abnormal child who is otherwise healthy and strong. She does not give to anyone else the duty of taking care of it. Twenty or thirty times a day she, without complaint, attends to this poor fruit of her womb, but a time will come when she can no longer do so. Then it is that she will look for someone to take her place in this heroic service. Let us not throw a stone at her unless we ourselves, and for many years, have had the experience of this sublime love. One day she takes with her her poor child to one of the little known homes where these human wrecks are assembled. For the last time she covers him with kisses and goes away sobbing. A religious is there; ten times a year but without ever becoming accustomed to it, she weeps with the poor unfortunate mother and welcomes this new child in her family which is so numerous and seemingly loved with such futility. Fifteen hours a day and without a vacation—she does not have the courage to take one since her poor little "prisoners" have none—this mother established in heroism will remain there for twenty-five and even forty years. She must feed these greedy little mouths and keep clean the room where this sad group wanders about with haggard eyes. On the day of her jubilee, one of these religious (for in the Church they are numbered by hundreds) said to some of her poor children still capable of understanding and who had wished her a happy feast:

"I have often said I have had my reward here below. I do not think I could have had a life more beautiful than that which I have had among you. To succeed in life (said Sister Colette) is to remain untouched until the end. Virginity—that is it." [30]

But in our great human family we can count wretched members descended so low in misfortune that they could never understand such a comparison.

Near beds where lie the most wretched of the race there still comes from the Heart of God that pity through which a religious, unsuspected by the multitude, makes herself a faithful messenger by day or night.

It is a very humble place which this mass of flesh incapable of lucid thought occupies on earth (except in the heart of its mother and sometimes not always there). The sister takes the hand of this poor being and feels sometimes a pressure in response. Is it a feeling or only the instinctive reaction of the poorest toward love? The ambassadress of the tenderness of God renews unwearyingly her appeal; the only movement which this human wreck might perceive, and in a way which remains mysterious to us.

The auxiliaries of the Good Shepherd

They move about discreet and silent, a well-used rosary slipping through their roughened hands. Living in the intimacy of Christ, Whose kindness they show forth faithfully, they let themselves be guided blindly toward the persons preferred by their Master. They take up their positions near many unhappy people drawn together in sorrow, distress, often in shame, and habitually in solitude. Here there is a girl scarcely twenty-five years old. One can see that she had been very beautiful. Her beauty plunged her into wretchedness. Vice has faded her youthful face, ravaged its features. Her parents have disinherited her, sent her out, and cursed her. She has no longer any friends. She has known what it is to be in prison. She is there awaiting the end of her broken and miserable life. She is beset by shame, bitterness, rancor, and hatred. Sleep would be to her a welcome refuge, but she cannot sleep. By the light of a candle, she sees approaching one who has never treated her with contempt. That night for the first time she did not turn her eyes away from the crucifix. Understandingly she looks at that other disfigured face and she weeps. By the smile which follows the tears, the humble religious understands that her cry has been heard and that Christ comes one more time "to save that which was lost." [31] Without saying anything, her pure lips touch the forehead which a mother has sworn never to kiss again. This maternal gesture added to so many others has not exhausted her great love. Disciple of the Virgin who is the consoler of the afflicted and refuge of sinners, the humble night watcher continues her nocturnal pilgrimage through the large rooms and, again resembling the Mother of Jesus, she keeps "all these things in her heart." [32] Each one of these beds from which for thirty years have passed so many sick people recalls to her many things. She has the impression in her memory and her faithful heart of having lived hundreds of lives, of having dried rivers of tears, of having averted thousands of revolts. With her soul full of gratitude, she thanks God Who has associated her so intimately with His kindness.

Sisters of the prisons

In the descending hierarchy of hatred and contempt, it seems that we ought to give the lowest degree to those who inhabit prisons and jails. When they leave the courtroom where the justice of men has condemned them, often the raging crowds have shouted for their deaths. Their guards snatch them from a society which rejects and curses them with jeers and the most scornful words in the language. They enter the courtyard and then the enclosure where there is no longer earthly mercy and pardon. But in a house now marked with shame a poor mother looks long at the portrait of her prisoner son. Her frequent tears remain a testimony of her fidelity during long years. The poor woman kisses lovingly the picture of the most unhappy of her children. It is her last maternal gesture.

Religious have known and felt that the most unfortunate of men, as well as the sick or the old, should never be abandoned by all. These are the children of God, the brothers of Christ Who has shared their lot, for He said: "I was a prisoner." [33] And it is to faithful religious that He will say in front of all mankind at the last Judgment, "You came to visit Me." They remain mothers and sisters of prisoners and more often than one thinks the final Judge makes, on this earth, their love and their resignation turn to real sanctity.

The proof seems very well established and difficult to deny that chastity can make religious more heroic and more faithful than mothers according to the flesh.

The Church remains holy and living. The chastity of her religious is the permanent channel in which the great stream of the kindness of God flows forward to the world of souls. Their sincere virtues are employed in many apostolates. Upright souls observe, weigh, and judge them; and a longing arises in their hearts for the perfection of the Heavenly Father. Some of them get away from their commonplace and monotonous faults; some detach themselves from egotism, vain rivalries, and sterile hatreds. They divine that there must exist another world, another universe, which is inhabited by pure beings so very kind to all their brothers. A world of souls is guided on its way by the lamp of the wise virgins. The religious themselves thank God for having chosen them to make His love known to children and to the sick, to be at the bedside of the rejected and the wrecks of our race, to be near the victims of folly or the vices of men. They are grateful to God Who has chosen them to remain as voluntary prisoners, near more unhappy but not the least loved of the children. They thank God for having placed them on the path which forced them to proceed toward greatness, heroism, and sanctity, and which will open at the end to the splendor of God. "Blessed are the pure of heart, for they shall see God." [34]

[1] I Cor., 7-34.

[2] **Spiritual Relations, Avila,** 19th of Jan., 1572.

[3] I St. John, 14-16.

[4] Eph., III, 18.

[5] Psalms, XXI, 9-11.

[6] Psalms, XXVI, 10.

[7] Sirach, IV, 10.

[8] Isaias, LXVI, 12-13.

[9] Osee, II, 21-22.

[10] Psalms, CXXXVIII, 7-10.

[11] Exodus, XXXIII, 11.

[12] I Chron., X, 9.

[13] Psalms, LXXI, 17.

[14] Psalms, CI, 26-28.

[15] Psalms, LXX, 9.

[16] Psalms, LXX, 9 to 18.

[17] Isaias, LIV, 10.

[18] Psalms, XXII, 9.

[19] Sirach, XVIII, 12.

[20] St. Luke, XVIII, 22.

[21] Phil., IV, 7.

[22] Way of Perfection, Ch. XXIV.

[23] Ibid., Ch. VII.

[24] St. Luke, I, 38.

[25] St. John, II, 5.

[26] I Thess., II, 7-8.

[27] Psalms, XXVI, 1.

[28] St. Mark, X, 30.

[29] Madame de Sévigne to Madame de Grignan: "Maternal love is violent."

[30] de Greef: The night is my Light.

[31] St. Matt., XVIII, 11.

[32] St. Luke, II, 19.

[33] St. Matt., XXV, 36.

[34] St. Matt., V, 8.

CHAPTER IV

OBEDIENCE

To OBEY is . . . to REIGN

Placed between the obedience of Christ and the submission and slavery of a great part of the human race, our religious obedience takes on a superb meaning and can play a magnificent role.

The "Servant of Jehovah" is Christ the King. The "Handmaid of the Lord" has been proclaimed Queen of the World. They are royal and yet they obeyed. We participate in their royalty in sharing their obedience.

Ever a worthy teacher, Jesus, after giving us the theory of obedience, showed us to what great lengths the obedience proposed to us should go. Our efforts make us tend to understand more fully the thought of our Model. We strive to make our acts of obedience, which are often difficult and sometimes heroic, approach the goal Jesus shows us: He died in obeying.

The submission of our Leader has given a meaning and a value to all human servitude. Following the example of our Guide, we dream, in the measure that it is possible, of giving a meaning and a value to all the forms of servitude existing in all countries, to the slavery of all ages.

I. JESUS, MODEL OF OUR OBEDIENCE

"Hail, King of the Jews." [1]

Jesus said one day:

> "You know that the rulers of the Gentiles lord it over
> them, and their great men exercise authority over them.
> Not so is it among you. On the contrary, whoever wishes
> to become great among you shall be your servant; and
> whoever wishes to be first among you shall be your slave;
> even as the Son of Man has not come to be served but to
> serve, and to give his life as a ransom for many." [2]

After the doctrine, come the application and the example. It was at the exact moment when Jesus had descended to
the lowest degree of abjection, when His diadem was a crown
of thorns, His royal mantle a rag, His scepter a reed, that
slaves proclaimed Him their sovereign, "Hail, King of the
Jews." At the top of the Cross His royalty was proclaimed in
the three languages known to the crowds who were insult-
ing Him.[3] They challenged Him to come down from the
Cross.[4] He did nothing of the kind, for His Will was to abase
Himself, "taking the nature of a slave . . . becoming obedient to death." [5]

At the moment that our Leader expired, His Mother was
present in virtue of the promise made at the time of the
Incarnation, "Behold the Handmaid of the Lord." [6]

When Jesus breathed out His soul into the hands of His
Father, Mary received His last sigh and as a mother associated herself with His heroic obedience. Jesus from now on
is fully entitled to be called the king of the obedient. No

one else has descended so low in submission. No one could equal Him in the perfection of His obedience:

> "Sacrifice or oblation you wished not, but ears open to obedience you gave me. Holocausts or sin-offerings you sought not; then said I, 'Behold I come; in the written scroll it is prescribed for me, to do your will, O my God, is my delight, and your law is within my heart!' " [7]

In the face of the almost universal subjection of human beings, our loyal Master could not leave to one of His human brethren the lowest place in the world of slaves; He reserved it for Himself. In His divine knowledge, Christ was ignorant of none of the sufferings endured by the great crowds of the obedient throughout the centuries. The cries and sobs of slaves, victims of the most barbarous cruelty, found an echo in His Heart.

It is because He alone can have complete knowledge of all forms of servitude that Christ knew to what depths His own must descend in order to reach the lowest degree. Our Lord has been able to gather together and live in His obedience all the submission ever experienced by the human race. The comparison made of the attitude of the Incarnate Word in the face of death with that of the rest of mankind can be repeated for all Christ's feelings and states of mind.

> "Fear of death is a universal feeling that is clothed in many forms, many of which are assuredly beyond the scope of human language. There is only one man who has known them all, and that was Christ in His agony." [8]

Isaias contemplating our Savior said, "Surely he has borne our iniquities and carried our sorrows." [9]

If our Lord has had St. Paul transmit to us this brotherly command, "Bear one another's burdens," [10] it is because He first of all proclaimed Himself our companion, walking along the same paths and bowed down under the same yoke.[11]

At the source and at the base of our Master's teaching, there is an elementary but essential principle, a definitive attitude to be taken and a spirit to be assimilated. St. Augustine had the gift of presenting clearly to us our Lord's thought:

> "Place yourself in my school; I shall not teach you how to create a world; I shall not reveal to you how to draw from nothingness things visible and invisible . . . I shall not teach you to scatter miracles nor to raise the dead. Take a place at the foot of my rostrum, because I am a Doctor in the science of making men meek." [12]

This is the Master whose disciples we wish to be

Our dreams and our desires carry us towards an always more faithful and sincere imitation.

Following His example, we wish to be inspired by all the acts and states of submission we encounter.

In order not to follow our Guide at too great a distance, we strive with His grace to rise even to heroic submission.

Stimulating our own obedience

In the first page of her "life written by herself," St. Teresa of Avila gives us this information about her father:

> "My father was a man of great charity towards the poor,

*Let St. Dominic Savio be your guide.
He is your classroom patron.*

and compassion for the sick, and also for servants; so
much so, that he never could be persuaded to keep slaves,
for he pitied them so much; and a slave belonging to
one of his brothers being once in his house, was treated
by him with as much tenderness as his own children. He
used to say that he could not endure the pain of seeing
that she was not free." [13]

We do not know whether there exists a study that brings
out the influence exercised on the religious obedience of the
great Reformer of Carmel by the memory of the slaves she
met in her youth. When we know her greatness of soul, it
is impossible for us to doubt that the sad fate of these pitiable
beings singularly stimulated her virtue. She could not forget
the counsel of God Himself not to oppress the slave but to
"remember that thou also wast a bondservant in the land of
Egypt and the Lord thy God made thee free." [14]

We know more of the celebrated Prioress' passion to
serve drawn from the great love produced in her by the
contemplation of Jesus.

"When the soul remembers that it has never served Thee
at all, and that by living on it may do Thee some service,
it longs for a still heavier cross, and never to die before
the end of the world." [15]

The haunting thought of the
crowds who labor in subjection

When the cities throughout the world awake, crowds
rush towards many and varied places of work, urged on by
whistles, bells, and the shrieks of sirens. Many of them fear

the penalties imposed for being a few minutes late. Soon a whole people is busy with extremely varied tasks. All are subject to heads of workshops or construction yards, to foremen, to heads of offices or departments. These subordinates are in turn conscious of the fact that they themselves are watched and governed by directors, engineers, and owners. Think, too, of the crowds of pupils in the schools.

Many questions arise concerning the persons who have to be in such groups and who are forced to be submissive. What takes place in their hearts when they bend over their work? What feelings may not be seething in their souls! In a great number it is resignation, a kind of fatalism. If we often visit the lowly and the simple, we are astounded by their power and capacity of endurance.

In others, who are more clear-sighted and self-conscious, there is bitterness, rancor, interior rebellion against the dealings and injustice of which they feel themselves to be the powerless and innocent victims. When these sentiments are increased a few degrees there is unleashed in their hearts a torturing exasperation, especially when, to the crushing weight of forced subjection, their companions in work and misery add rough jokes, reproaches, unjust actions, sometimes cruelty and blows.

The meek—for all groups of humanity include them in greater or lesser numbers—have been dreaming for years of the dawn of a better world where justice will reign and kindness will prevail.

We find likewise, mingling with the crowds of workers, noble men and women who, for the most part, have been formed by Catholic Action, though some of them are consecrated beings.[16] All these have voluntarily chosen to share the common lot of the immense majority of mankind. With a clear vision, conscientiously and tactfully, these apostles and friends of the working classes so contrive that there will be nothing that they do not know about fatigue, about the monotony of always repeating the same gestures, and the uncertainty the poor suffer concerning the morrow. Above all, far from being satisfied with passing experiences after which they could find in comfort the liberty they have temporarily sacrificed, these apostles bind themselves even to "retirement" by promises, even by vows, which make them in all things like their brothers and sisters in work and trouble.

In the service of the city of men

The cities of men have their public services. Statisticians are busy foreseeing their needs, computing their resources, calculating their revenues. Day and night, watchers guard their security, ready to give an immediate signal if dangers, such as fire and floods, threaten them.

Privileged above others, we religious seek, with the pastors of souls, to increase and enrich the spiritual treasure of an entire people. We are invited to become the good Cyrenians of all those who no longer have the courage nor the strength to carry their heavy cross. We have only to believe in the mysteries of the supernatural world to know what a beneficial osmosis keeps us in vital contact, in symbiosis, with the great crowds of those who live in subjection. The most sensitive recorders, the instruments of the highest precision, photo-electric cells are only pale images and inadequate comparisons of the aptitudes that loving hearts have to receive the sufferings, the expectations and even the hopes of the unfortunate. The cries of the rebellious, the helpless tears of the humiliated, the aspirations towards the ideal, "the hunger and thirst after justice," [17] all these forces, in a strange but active interfusion, converge towards the hearts of us modern religious. This irreplaceable knowledge directs our apostolic enterprises, our labors, our devotedness. God, the universal Provider, makes use of our lives for the advantage of the people of whom we are at one and the same time the children, guides, and guardians.

Turning to account heroic obedience

For great needs there are great resources; for the overburdened, there is brotherly aid. An obedience that is material, easy and even joyful, could be only a feeble help to the incalculable number of those who are exasperated by monotonous occupations or who revolt against the work they detest and hate with passion.

Efficacious and successful help comes to them (by ways and means God keeps secret) from all the merits won by the psychological dramas brought about by the heartrending and heroic obedience of a certain number of religious. It is said rather frequently among us that in a fervent life an act of obedience requiring heroism will one day present itself. Spiritually, for the one concerned, it can be the royal gate opening upon sanctity. It is in these tragic hours that perhaps the quality and the outcome of our testimony are decided. It has been pertinently said:

> "The entire life of a man, I mean a man at a decisive turning-point in the history of humanity or of the Church, often depends on a single instant. To make their existence effective, these men have only a second. If they fail in it, they have failed in their whole life." [18]

In the wonderful world of supernatural success, the repercussions of this law can be prodigous. A crucifying act of obedience, at times the belated fruit of a vow made at the age of twenty, can come to the aid of hundreds of unfortunates who are prostrated and crushed by trials beyond their slender resources. It can likewise happen that the heroism of an hour is followed by disagreeable demands that are continually renewed. In greater numbers than we think, there are religious who each morning have to take up again a task they detest. The years pass, their repugnance remains and often increases. A painstaking exploration of the world of souls would end by revealing the existence of a law, namely, that trials are symmetric and synchronized.

Even after the advent of professional guidance, there remains among the working class a large number of those who acquit themselves of their work only because it gives them a living, though they literally find it repulsive. The least expert of guidance directors would have spared these pitiable victims those occupations for which they have no kind of aptitude. The repugnance they feel will remain a terrible fatality.[19]

The dramas of religious and lay persons meet therefore and are united in regions which are difficult to explore but in which the sufferings of religious can show abundant harvests. The rebellion of those who, like us, perform repugnant tasks can be appeased or eliminated, thanks to the contribution and compensation we bring in accepting duties that are at first distasteful but in the end loved.

When one believes with all his soul in the brotherhood of the unfortunate among themselves, when one has become a citizen in the kingdom of poverty, he yields to the need of coming to the aid of the most suffering and the most sorely tried in the great multitude of the afflicted. At the moment when an unknown brother was just about to be engulfed in despair, at the precise instant that he was preparing to commit suicide, there awakened in his heart (he would indeed be incapable of discovering how such a thought came to him) the idea of making himself, in his turn, helpful to others by offering up his afflictions.

Those men and women who have been crushed, but also transformed and greatly sanctified by heroic obedience, acquire new senses that allow them to explore unknown worlds. It has been said that there are things that are not seen except by eyes that have wept, and that there are wounds which, to be cured, need hands comparable to those of the Crucified. All the sciences are not imprisoned in our books and libraries. There are many that God uses to adorn the hearts of His friends, His chosen ones: the irreplaceable sciences of pity and compassion for the unfortunate are among them.

II. OUR OBEDIENCE CAN BE HELPFUL TO THE SLAVES OF ALL AGES

Religious women, because they are Catholic, daughters of the Father of mankind and very docile children of the Church, are obsessed by great facts in the history of mankind, and often they are perturbed and stimulated by them.

In order to renew and enrich our meditations on obedience, it may be profitable to consider other kinds of submission. Let us limit ourselves to recall three facts that have gigantic proportions:

the fact of slavery in antiquity;
the fact of the slave trade;

the dreadfully current fact of the millions of slaves in
our generation.

We shall try to see then how our religious obedience
could give a meaning, even a value, to all the types of subjection endured by our fellow human beings.

1. Slavery in ancient times

The history of millions of slaves does not exist. To survive
in the memory of man is a privilege and a certain kind of
wealth. How could we know the names and deeds of those
who were held in so little account by their masters? One
might denounce this crying injustice, but professional historians would answer that without documents, it would be
impossible to write history. The history of the slaves' sufferings, feelings and interior rebellion is now and then thought
of by generous souls, but it will never be anything but a
desire and a dream.[20]

We know, however, that the principle of slavery was
founded on a philosophy without pity. Aristotle has left us
these implacable formulas:

> "When there is such a difference as that between soul
> and body, or between men and animals, the lower sort
> are by nature slaves, and it is better for them as for all
> inferiors that they should be under the rule of a master.
> . . . It is clear then, that some men are by nature free,
> and others slaves, and that for these latter slavery is both
> expedient and right. . . .

"The use made of slaves and tame animals is not very different. . . . There is in some cases a marked distinction between the two classes, rendering it expedient and right for the one to be slaves and the other to be masters; the one practicing obedience, the other exercising the authority and lordship nature intended them to have.[21]

It is easy to imagine what conclusion could be drawn from such principles by those whom St. Paul knew so well and whom he described as "without affection and without pity." [22]

The recruiting of slaves was easy. A war was waged and the vanquished people fell into slavery. The conquerors did not hamper themselves with useless mouths. Women, children, the sick, the old, the wounded were killed on the spot. The final selection kept only the most vigorous of the able-bodied men. After the conquest of Gaul, Caesar brought back to Italy a million slaves.

These unfortunates were dispersed to the markets where there were "traffickers in men." [23] Ten thousand slaves were sold at Delos in a single day. The purchasers became the absolute masters of the slaves, having over them the right of life and death. They could kill ten a day, without having to render an account to anyone.

In the Roman and Greek worlds the immense majority of the population belonged to the servile class. Athens had only twenty thousand free citizens while she had four hundred thousand slaves. Historians estimated that Rome alone possessed a million slaves.

We can think how sorrowful must have been the lives of these poorest of the poor. When looking at the Colosseum,

almost all Christians recall the crowds of martyrs who
ascended towards the glory of Heaven from this vast relic
of past times.

However, it is not forbidden to think also of the thousands of slaves who, slowly and with immense suffering,
caused this marvelous building to rise towards the sky.
How many atrocious scenes were lived out in this immense
construction yard. As soon as dawn came, shouts called to
work all these laborers. How many of them had not slept,
being obsessed by their irremediable plight? Others shivered
with fever, and torn by coughs, spat blood. Every day a certain number fell, completely exhausted. Those in charge of
the work, armed with whips and clubs, finished them with
blows. Their bodies, consumed by the fires that were always
kept up, fell into ashes, and these, being thrown into the
sewer, found their way down the Tiber and then to the sea.
Their immortal souls are still ilving; what has become of
them? Those who today obey have the right to ask themselves this question. We shall say later what answer may
be proposed to this immense mystery.

2. The slave trade

Let us pass over some centuries and change continents.
Towards the year 1600 innocent tribes were hunting for
their living in the savannahs of Africa. One day mysterious
ships appeared on the horizon. The inoffensive groups who
were pursuing game were themselves soon hunted by men
with white faces.

Let us see them as they were collected on the shore in
ever larger groups. It needed many pursuits, and therefore

a certain amount of time, to collect enough for a cargo. Let us not be afraid to watch the sifting of these products of manhunts. The wounded and the poorly formed were finished on the spot. The rest were crammed into the hold of the vessel, for it was taken into account that it would be necessary to throw some into the sea as waste matter. Then came the departure towards a mysterious destiny, filled with terror. The corpses and those in their agony were thrown to the waves, where they were quickly seized and devoured by sharks.

After long weeks spent in crossing the ocean, the most robust survivors of the pitiless selection arrived in America. Fortunate were the ones who debarked at Carthagena in Colombia; a saint was waiting for them there. It was because he had helped, tended, consoled and loved 300,000 [25] of these deported negroes that St. Peter Claver, S.J., bears the enviable title of "Slave of the Blacks."

All these horrors and acts of cruelty are a little blurred by the mists of history, yet one can establish, not the details that cannot possibly be revived, but a rough balance sheet. It is known, for example, that from 1530 to 1800 almost ten million negroes

"were sent (from Africa) . . . to the other side of the Atlantic. An almost equal number died in the course of the march towards the African coast and in the warehouses."

"Bills of sale" have been published, showing that the sale of 450 slaves brought in a net profit of $390,000. With deep melancholy, one comes to the conclusion that

"One will never know the exact figures. No one will ever
be able to describe the sufferings and the monstrous
distress of these beings." [26]

Happy the religious who are obsessed by the thought of
the lot of these, their poor brethren. It is impossible to remain
mediocre in our obedience when we face an historic fact
of such scope. Those who are left indifferent by these horrible but past events can still find a permanent use for their
prayers and merits in applying them to the spiritual advantage of our own generation.

3.   The millions of slaves who are our contemporaries

If our compatriots can have a priority in our fraternal
assistance, it seems right that our contemporaries should
arouse our apostolic interest more than unknown persons
who have lived through their trials in other centuries. Let
us acknowledge, too, that religious as well as the faithful
give up all their merits through the mediation of the Blessed
Virgin. It seems to them that it would be lacking in a filial
spirit to express a desire and formulate a preference. God is
the incomparable distributor of our merits, and a certain
sense of service impels them to have a childlike and blind
confidence in Him.

But there are not wanting in every country religious who
are haunted, even to the point of anguish, by the lot of the
millions of slaves of our own generation. In the face of this
unchanging and world-wide tragedy there are apostles who,
without being able to consult one another, share the tasks
it imposes.

It appears to them all necessary and logical that at the

very time when entire peoples are reduced to slavery, those consecrated persons who have offered to God the holocaust of their liberty by their vow of obedience, should freely associate themselves with those constrained to obey. They claim their share in a suffering that has become so common.

God has heard the sincere prayer of His chosen children. In all the Churches of Silence, we count thousands of our brothers and sisters who often belong to our religious families, and who know all that is to be known about the suffering of so many modern slaves.[27] In construction yards, in mines, on farms, in workshops and factories, on dams, they share faithfully and lovingly the lot of their brothers and sisters in misery. A number of their unfortunate companions, who submit only because they are powerless to revolt, have hearts saturated with bitterness and exasperated by anger; [28] but the religious, sustained by the prayer always being offered for them in lands still free, savor their suffering and, under the eyes of God, give full value to the varied humiliations that come with total submission. Since they know and feel themselves the privileged children of the Universal Father, they train themselves to know all that can be endured in the most humiliating form of slavery.

The parable of the leaven and the flour is applicable to our generation as it was to its predecessors.[29] Mingled with the suffering multitudes, the slave-religious try to make this human mass rise towards Heaven. We know also that admirable Christians in the past succeeded in attaining real holiness by sharing and sanctifying the slavery of their brothers of the same race. Century after century, the Church adds new songs to the epic of her spiritual conquests.

From the earliest times of Christian history, the innumerable bands of martyrs included many slaves. Such happenings continue to be renewed.

Religious who really live their obedience in the midst of people passionately attached to liberty, understand better the meaning and the scope of their vow. They contrive in every way to have their part in the slavery endured by a good third of the human race. They firmly believe that, by being always more perfectly obedient and submissive, they can, in a small measure, aid in procuring strength, courage, peace, if not joy, for all the slaves in the world today. They have often noticed, and frequently heard others make the avowal, that the poor feel a useless increase of pain and humiliation when they see an insolent display of luxury that challenges their poverty. Religious therefore, at least a good number of them, feel strongly that to dream of independence and liberty at the very time when millions of slaves are suffering would not be worthy of them nor of their Master, the Divine Slave, Who died on the cross.

How can we give a meaning, and if possible, a value to all forms of slavery?

Our apostolic dreams and desires turn from the crowds of those now living in slavery to other perspectives. God alone holds the knowledge of the dramas experienced by immortal souls and He alone can measure their extent, yet these can sound a sorrowful echo and an "appeal" in the hearts of thousands of obedient religious.

Certain ones among them wonder with anguish whether it is really forbidden to give a meaning, or even a redemptive value to "the monstrous distress" of the victims of all forms of tyranny, and of the slaves of every century, not excepting

those before the Christian era. To souls of good will and to
those who are passionately interested in the apostolate, wide
horizons have been opened up by the research of theologians. They speak to us now of the "The Retroactive Effects
of Prayer."[30]

God, Who sees all in an eternal present, can bring about
that the prayer of a religious of the twentieth century could
benefit the souls of her very distant ancestors who lived in
the fifteenth or even the tenth century.

> "The passion of Christ had a retroactive effect in offering
> the means of salvation to men who lived before our Chris-
> tian era. Why would it not be the same with our prayers,
> which are known in advance by the Father of Mercy? [31]

Relying on this opinion which has been declared "very
acceptable" by Abbe A. Michel, one of the best qualified
historians of theology, we took the liberty of asking him
this other question: since prayer can have retroactive effects,
why could not the obedience of modern religious, in a way
that will always remain deeply mysterious, give a meaning
and even a value to the oppression and slavery inflicted for
thousands of years upon so many of our brothers in humanity?

Without entering into all the details of a statement that
is as technical as it is authoritative, we quote the conclusions
of the encouraging reply.

> "Theoretically . . . the affirmative could be defended;
> on one essential condition, however, that those men of
> epochs anterior to Christianity died—perhaps aided by
> their suffering—in Divine friendship. One knows all the

problems raised by the grave and agonizing question of the salvation of the infidel . . .

". . . in what measure do these graces obtain their effect, in what numbers did the infidels before our era attain salvation? . . . A mystery, a mystery . . . nevertheless, a mystery that does not forbid us to think of those men and women who can be assimilated to them. . . .[32]

Theologically then it is permitted us to hope that our obedience, sought, freely accepted, and long prepared for in the novitiate, allows us to play a "cosmic" role in the magnificent world of souls. Obedience has a special redemptive value. It is because Christ

"humbled himself, becoming obedient unto death, even to death on a cross. Therefore God also has exalted him and has bestowed on him the name that is above every name, so that at the name of Jesus every knee should bow of those in heaven, on earth and under the earth, and every tongue should confess that the Lord Jesus Christ is in the glory of God the Father."[33]

Among all holocausts that of obedience is, according to the very words of God, the most decisive and the one that most reveals the sincerity of our hearts. At the precise moment when Abraham blindly obeyed the command of the Most High, when he was lifting his sword to immolate his only son, Isaac, he heard this assurance:

"Now I know that thou fearest God, because thou hast not spared thine only-begotten son."[34]

St. Ignatius, in his letter on obedience, teaches us that this virtue is "a kind of holocaust by which the entire man unreservedly sacrifices himself in the flames of charity to his Creator and Lord." [35]

Of the three passions sacrificed by our vows, love of liberty and independence seems the most deeply rooted in the hearts of the men of today. For some decades now we can count by the millions the men and women who have literally sacrificed all in the hope of remaining free. They have abandoned their goods and their families, in certain cases, persons whom they passionately loved; many have fled even from their beloved country that they had served with all their strength.

Before the cross of our Model Who died through obedience, and in the face of our contemporaries, so passionately attached to their freedom, our obedience takes on meaning and plays a role. Every day, and sometimes several times a day, we must renew the sacrifice of our independence and of our freedom. However, we believe that our acts of obedience, which are difficult and sometimes heroic, have beneficial repercussions.

The liturgy of Lent has us sing:

"Bury your alms in the breast of the poor; from there it will cry to God in your favor. For, just as water extinguishes fire, alms efface sin." [36]

Much is revealed to us by this attractive promise. In order to render our obedience always more efficacious for our fellow human beings, we shall seek to make it closer to the harshest types of subjection and less unworthy of the most barbarous slavery. After this "success," we can expect that God will say to us, as to His servant Abraham, that He is now sure of our sincerity.

As beloved children of the Father of Heaven, we plead at His tribunal the cause of our unfortunate brethren.

If an alms is sufficient to efface sins, we dare to hope that the heroism of our obedience will be our filial way of invoking God and of imploring His pity for the horrible crime which consists in robbing entire peoples of their freedom and of subjugating masses of human beings.

Confiding in the goodness and infinite mercy of our Father, and knowing His need to have pity on all of us, we dare hope also that our voluntary submission, laden with our ever increasing love, will appease and eliminate the feelings of revolt in aching hearts.

Believing in the indescribable osmosis brought about by the loving wisdom of the Lord, we direct "the incense of glory" that comes from the holocaust of our obedience, to the throne of His infinite majesty, asking at the same time that sanctity will arise, flourish, and bear fruit in the wretched world of slaves.[36]

[1] St. Matthew, XXVII, 29.

[2] Ibid., XX, 25-28.

[3] Ibid., XXVII, 39.

[4] Ibid., 40.

[5] Philippians, II, 6-8.

[6] St. Luke, I, 38.

[7] Psalms, XXXIX, 7-9.

[8] Georges Bernanos, 1888-1948.

[9] Isaias, LIII, 4.

[10] Galatians, VI, 2.

[11] St. Matthew, XI, 29-30.

[12] Patrologie Latine, XXXVIII, 443. Cf. Common of Abbots.

13 **Autobiography,** Ch. I.

14 Deuteronomy, XV, 15.

15 **Autobiography,** Ch. XVI.

16 This is the case and lot of certain "Secular Institutes." Cf. Monseigneur Guyot, Bishop of Coutances: **The Religious Life,** Pastoral Letter, Lent, 1959, p. 8, note 14. Cf. Codex Can., 487 and the following. The Secular Institutes constitute a state of perfection, but they are specifically different from the religious life. Cf. J. M. Perrin: **Consecration to God and Presence in the World.** Desclee de Brouwer.

17 St. Matthew, V, 6.

18 G. Théry, O.P., Catherine de Francheville, Foundress at Vannes of the First House of Retreat for Women. (1620-1689).

19 See our **Awakeners of Souls.** Society of St. Paul, N. Y., 1957, p. 197.

20 G. K. Chesterton was inconsolable about this.

21 **Politics,** Book I, Ch. 2.

22 Romans, I, 31.

23 I Timothy, I, 10.

24 Dictionnaire Théologie Catholique. "Slavery," col. 457-458. All the facts cited here are mentioned in this article.

25 Figure cited in the Bull of his canonization.

26 Hans Leip: **Le Roman du Gulf-Stream,** 1956, pp. 119-120. Club des Libraires de France.

27 It is logical and just to add to "the slaves" of totalitarian regimes the innumerable individuals who, though working in "free" countries, feel and consider themselves "enslaved."

28 It is said, however, that some wear themselves out joyfully, happy in the thought that they are bequeathing to following generations a world that will be better organized materially.

29 St. Matthew, XIII, 33.

30 **L'Ami du Clergé,** 1953, pp. 104-105.

31 A. Michel: **Mystéres de l'Au-delà.** Tequi, Paris, p. iii.

23 **L'Ami du Clergé,** 1956, p. 421.

33 Philippians, II, 8-11.

34 Genesis, XXII, 12.

35 **Letter,** paragraph 9.

36 Saturday of Ember Week, Third Lesson, response.

CHAPTER V

THE COMMON LIFE

> "Behold how good it is and how
> pleasant where brethren dwell at
> one." [1]

All the friends of God who know the Bible feel that there exists as it were a parallelism, a sort of similarity, between the above affirmation and the text which was sung by the communicants of the first Christian ages: "Taste and see how good the Lord is. Happy the man who takes refuge in Him." [2]

The faithful, children like ourselves of the same Heavenly Father, are aware of our joys. They arouse in them a longing for a community life and their fraternal intuition gives them some idea of its advantages. Children of the same Church, they have a right to know the triumph of our Mother. Certainly, they need to do so. In the unending list of our joys, let us set before them these simple advantages:

1st—The common life insures for us kind and understanding superiors.

2nd—The Constitutions and Rules point out to us the Will of God.

3rd—In accepting the difficulties and obediences of a life lived in common, we are enabled to experience

the greatest of human sufferings and to make ourselves good Cyrenians to many of our contemporaries
who are crushed by crosses too heavy for their feeble shoulders.

I. "PRIVILEGES" OF SUPERIORS ARE ADVANTAGES FOR INFERIORS

Old texts call superiors "vicars of God." This beautiful
title condenses and sums up a whole tradition. In the community, the superior is the living image of the Heavenly
Father. In whatever way superiors are chosen, whether by
election or nomination by a major authority, their subjects
consider them the envoys and representatives of God. The
respect which surrounds an abbot and the sincere love that
religious women have for their Mother (they often call her
"the good Mother," "our dear Mother," or "our Mother")
cannot be explained nor understood without the above viewpoint. Many biblical texts show these transpositions and easy
and obvious applications. How many superiors have drawn
from these inspired formulas the profoundest knowledge in
the art of governing.

> "Sovereignty over the earth is in the Hand of God Who
> raises up on it the man of the hour; sovereignty over
> every man is in the Hand of God, Who imparts His
> majesty to the ruler." [3]

A sure instinct calls together the flock around the shepherd, the chosen one of God.

> "And all the earth desired to see Solomon's face, to hear
> his wisdom which God had given him in his heart." [4]

Familiar with the sacred texts through their incessant meditation, the members of a community have read joyfully the instructions given by God in person to His "vicars."

> "Tend ye the flock of God which is among you, govern-
> ing not under constraint but willingly according to God;
> nor yet for the sake of base gain, but eagerly; nor yet as
> lording it over your charges, but becoming from the
> heart a pattern to the flock." [5]

The spirit of faith invites us to think and believe that the Almighty, an infinitely wise distributor, bestows on each superior the qualities and gifts which will render him better able to exercise his charge:

> "But all these things are the work of one and the same
> spirit Who allots to each one what He will." [6]

Founded on a confidence of which the source is in God, obedience as well as submission can become easier because it is filial.

> "Obey your superiors and be subject to them for they
> keep watch as having to render an account of your souls
> so that they do this with joy and not with grief for that
> would not be expedient for you." [7]

> "Now we beseech you, brethren, to appreciate those who
> labor among you and who are over you in the Lord and
> admonish you." [8]

"Privileges" of Superiors

It is the singular "privilege" of superiors to have been chosen by God to become His substitutes among the many beautiful souls which it pleases Him to call to our religious families. It is a fact that frequently superiors are little known to outsiders. Their primary and most important role is to sanctify the souls of their subjects, to awaken their ideals, to direct their apostolates, activities which scarcely draw the attention of the great public. On the contrary, all that matters to them in the course of centuries is to be the first confidants of sometimes magnificent projects. They are kind listeners to books destined to be famous. Again, theirs is the task of sustaining the first steps of their subjects on the route of their marvelous apostolates. It has been given to them to witness in amazement great progress in the Kingdom of God.

Superiors assist at the unfolding of superb projects

It was under the eyes and sometimes under the inspiration of the abbots of our old monasteries that the plans of the monasteries which today still are the principal pride of our old cities of Christianity were designed and corrected. The solid explanations which they laid before their monks on the attributes and the transcendance of our great and holy God remain there turned to stone. Under majestic and age-old vaults the power, grandeur, beauty and sanctity of the Creator have always been exalted. These structures, sometimes in building for two or three centuries,[9] called forth the tenacity and perseverance of a succession of superiors, upholders of the ideal, who reanimated courage and who were always open to ingenious discoveries or to daring suggestions. But how can we find the personal part, the mark of a certain father on the work of sons who in some cases were endowed with genius. Their perfection as a whole, admired and envied by our technicians, is a permanent proof of the fruitfulness of a collaboration between subjects and their father.

Superiors are able to look for the development of immortal works

There is another world still more beautiful but much more difficult to explore. What was the individual part of the superiors in the inspiration or the composition of the many books written in religious communities? Among abbots, guardians, priors, and superiors, such and such a one has left imperishable works. The leaders and founders of schools go from St. Anselm to St. Bonaventure, from St. Ignatius of Loyola to St. Alphonsus Liguori, from St. Vincent de Paul to St. Grignon de Montfort, from St. Gertrude to St. Teresa of Avila. But how many others, absorbed by their multiple tasks, never succeeded in writing a book although they dreamed of doing it all their lives. Some of them live on through one of their subjects who has interpreted their own thoughts. The cleverest as well as the most subtle critics can never determine to what degree we are indebted for immortal masterpieces to priors who are completely unknown. Do we even know the names of the priors of St. Thomas Aquinas or St. John of the Cross? These very humble religious who have not left any trace in history were the first readers of the pages of the *Summa Theologica,* of the *Ascent of Carmel,* of the *Spiritual Canticle,* and of the *Living Flame of Love.* It is even possible that their judicious remarks have been of value in these developments from which many souls for many centuries have drawn ever increasing light and fervor. What an inestimable advantage for a writer, even if he be a future doctor of the Church, to have had a very kind father, a faithful image of the Eternal Light, to listen to him, encourage him, and sometimes inspire him. Christ in the Tabernacle was certainly not the only one to thank the Angelic Doctor for having written so well of Him. All the successive priors have had to express in the name of the Church the gratitude of many souls to the greatest of theologians.

Superiors are at the beginnings of great apostolates

Without even leaving their desks, superiors give life to apostolates carried on in many continents. From the little room in Rome,[10] St. Ignatius by his letters supported St. Francis Xavier in the long apostolic travels which took him from India to Japan, then to the coast of China. He also gave the commission to St. Peter Canisius, one of the great apostles to Germany. About the same time also, St. Teresa of Avila was having the Carmelites pray that many countries of Europe might be protected against heresy.

In receiving the blessing of their Abbot or Mother as they take their departure, religious missionaries have understood the scope of the task that has been confided to them. The epic of modern Catholic Missions cannot be understood, either in its spirit or its triumphs, if one does not take into account all the elements of its innumerable cantos. It is in the hearts of many superiors, more obscure than their sometimes illustrious subjects, that we shall have to go to find the sure source of the conquest of millions of souls. The apostolate depends in large part on the sanctity of the apostles, on their spirit as well as their zeal, but all this wealth comes from humble rooms inhabited by the inspirers of such a vast missionary apostolate: our thousands of superiors.

Superiors are the artisans of sanctity

Aware of the beauty as well as the greatness of their task, humble superiors know and feel that the principal end of their mission is to cause sanctity to flourish in the souls for whom they are, at the same time, mothers, guides, and models.

Their role has for them numerous "advantages." Their charge puts them in the position of seeing at close range, and often, many wonders in the world of souls. They collaborate with generous spiritual advancements.

Not all superiors are St. Gertrude nor St. Teresa of Avila, neither are they other St. Clares of Assisi. The offices of the Mothers of a Community do not always shelter a St. Jeanne de Chantal, a St. Madeleine-Sophie Barat, a blessed Mother d'Youville, or a beloved Mother Theodore Guérin. It is permissible, however, to hope that the time will come when admirable superiors, now living, will be numbered with St. Marie-Madeleine Postel, St. Euphrasie Pelletier, St. Francis Xavier Cabrini, and Maria Lopez Vicuna.

A long and varied experience suffices to convince one that remarkable things happen and are dreamed each day in the humble and poor rooms where superiors throughout the world receive continually thousands of disciples and subjects. It is the unceasing procession of the "privileged ones" of the Father of all souls. The younger religious outline their desires and the dreams of sanctity which made them renounce an attractive human love to abandon themselves to the good pleasure of God, to total dedication to their brethren, the afflicted and the poor. These manifest joys, shining forth, and enjoyed to the full, confirm the Mothers in the certitude that the King of the World is "the God Who gives joy and happiness." [11]

It is towards superiors of teaching Sisters, of nurses, of visitors of the sick poor, that reports of the noblest kind converge: concerning foundlings, the incurable, the humiliated, and persons overwhelmed with misfortune, ruin, and dishonor. There is not one of these Mothers, witness of so many beautiful things, to whom one needs to recall and point out that the Church always remains holy; that little ones and the poor, children and the unfortunate keep its spirit, and continue to bring to the treasury of the Communion of Saints riches comparable to those which were deposited there by their ancestors. An identical spirit and an inexhaustible strength continue to exalt and enlarge the human soul. How truly can the gratified and amazed superiors say: "I no longer need 'to believe' . . . I see God, Christ, our Lady, the Church; I watch them constantly at work in the beautiful universe of souls."

The superiors not only receive, but they give, sustain, inspire, and animate. They endeavor not to disappoint the expectations of the many souls eager for perfection and sanctity. Experience, more than any other activity, continually improves the government of superiors in the interests of souls.

When one has had the privilege of encouraging the hearts of many religious women of communities in many nations for more than a quarter of a century, it is easy to become convinced of certain obvious facts. God is the Friend, the Father, the marvelous Spouse of dedicated and surrendered souls. Triumphing over earthly dialects, the children of the Kingdom speak the same language: that of the eternal Gospel; that which our Lord taught on the Mount of the Beatitudes. That language, as well as that knowledge, makes minds and souls uniform. Those who know this doctrine, those who have grasped all its distinctions (and how many Mothers are wise in this domain!) have the gift and the secret of making their disciples progress in the way of spiritual infancy, and of docility to the Church.

Superiors communicate and circulate their discoveries. Their disciples, instructed, formed, and marked by them become, in the hands of God, flexible workers and faithful sowers of seed in the fields which the Creator has confided to them. There are superiors who, in obscurity and patience, prepare the apostles that the modern world subconsciously expects. Mistresses of Novices and of Junior Sisters strive to free their disciples from their passions and from their too human reactions. They communicate a fraternal instinct to them, an instinct which will drive away all preference for persons, which breaks through the caste spirit, does away with all forms of false patriotism and racial distinctions. The beneficiaries of these initial and solid formations become enriched with a mentality which is never lost, so much does it become a part of their being. Years may increase, duties, employments, and apostolates may vary, but it is possible to meet certain religious who remain unaffected by routine and doubt into which habit may often lead. The spectacle of common poverty and of human weakness spread about so universally can never make these souls, instructed by holy and fervent Mothers, become disillusioned, indifferent, and embittered. It is with an ever-increasing knowledge of hearts, with a zeal which nothing seems to lessen, that they approach the wrecks of humanity, slaves of their frailty or vices, still to be met in widely spread apostolates. In the depths of their hearts, they have anchored the ineradicable conviction that prayer and voluntary suffering for sinners are always efficacious. They know by sure knowledge, often confirmed by experience, that the poorest and the weakest of the family of Christians keep the hearts of children deep within themselves for God and our Lady.

And thus it is that humble superiors, often unknown in the town where they have lived a long time, are the inspirers, the promoters and the supporters of the apostolate of hundreds of religious, dispersed over many continents.

II. THE CONSTITUTIONS AND THE RULE

In receiving the book of the Constitutions of her Order, a young religious can say quite often and with great confidence: "These pages have been written by a great friend of God. They have transformed and sanctified lives by the thousands."

Since God called souls and invited them to seek perfection, He chose guides for them, and, through these, He states His Will clearly.

"We are happy, O Israel, because the things that are pleasing to God are made known to us." [12]

For the privileged ones of His flock, the eternal Shepherd

selects the best of His shepherds. He brings them into the group of His intimates:

> "The Lord used to speak to Moses, face to face, as one man speaks to another." [13]

This is the manner of God with the writers of Rules. He admits them to His intimacy, familiarizes them with His way of thinking. He strips them of their too human views. Through contemplation, unceasingly resumed, becoming almost habitual, directed and oriented by Truth Himself, their attention and enthusiasm are carried toward and concentrated on a Divine attribute. On the other hand, our legislators participating in immense love and in infinite mercy, find themselves unresisting, holily obsessed by a keen vision of human suffering, weakness, and moral decay. And steadily in a reciprocating motion of this ardent gaze, the writer is carried easily to God, but brought back to his writing, and thus penetrates and grasps better the Will of God. Little by little, the text is outlined, is perfected, and becomes our Rule.[13] God gives intuitions, arouses desires, and makes clear the surest means of realizing His wishes. Moreover, it sometimes happens that the Founders have only to summarize their personal experience,[14] their rapid progress toward God, in order to bring into focus the precious principles of the pathway that leads to the marvelous country of a Father loved and possessed.

The evident fervor of some religious families comes in direct line from the words and helps of the great friends of the Lord. There is a security in following the footsteps of such guides. The heavenly Friend specifies His wishes to His privileged ones. With maternal loyalty these religious trainers transmit them to their children. Less fervency tends to minimize the divine commands. Sanctity delivers its disciples from the sterility of mere words, from the triviality of mere gestures.

Plato assures us that

"Human laws are the discovery of the good legislators of the past." [15]

We have the conviction that our own laws have an origin still more sublime, and there has been given to us the power of judging them by their fruits. Followed with exactitude, the laws of a city make good citizens; well lived, our Constitutions have sanctified generations of religious. From Saint Teresa of Avila down to fervent religious still living the agreement is unanimous:

"I tried to think what I could do for God, and thought that the first thing was to follow my vocation to a religious life which His Majesty had given me by keeping my Rule with the greatest perfection possible." [16]

Those in our communities say the same thing. With what simplicity and confidence thousands of religious repeat unceasingly, without being tired or discouraged, the appeals of the Psalm with which they are familiar:

"Good and upright is the Lord; thus He shows sinners the way. . . . Your ways make known to me, teach me your paths; guide me in your truth and teach me, for you are my God and my Savior." [17]

We thank God and His Church for having made so many pathways converge towards happiness. It does not require a great spirit of faith to be uplifted at this sight. Coming from the heart of God, uttered by His friends, the multiple calls have been sent out to souls of all races and all tongues. The Will of God makes itself flexible and adaptable to mentalities and civilizations. It has known how to take sensibilities and possibilities into account . . . showing patience to the sheep and the lambs who have long marches to make. Then, little by little, rich and varied elements commence to amalgamate within these same groups. Barriers are broken down, souls respond to the same call, share the same ideal, and learn all languages in order to relieve with more efficacy poverty and its multiform distresses. So universal are they that they have no longer a nationality nor a country.

Coming from all parts of the earth, and going to all continents, religious families are united in the same love, are called together to the house of the same Father.

Remarkable variety of patronal names of communities

It is in the varied vocations given by an infinitely holy God, and in the goodness, mercy, and compassion which He causes to flourish in the hearts of many Foundresses in every country that one must seek for the source of the profusion of patronal titles under which our thousands of Congregations of women are known. We see in them nothing which is simply originality, confusion, caprice, or picturesqueness, when we set ourselves to reconstruct the synthesis and the philosophy underlying the choice. It is easy to see in it the various forms of praise, and one especially, solicitous to be given lavishly in aid and compassion to the unlimited aspects of human suffering.

God, "the first to be served," is honored and glorified

in every way, in the Trinity as well as in its attributes. Christ and the Blessed Virgin have found singers and servants of their mysteries. The Saints of all races are already or will become the patrons of religious families whose number is always increasing.

Therefore, the Trinity, the Eternal Father, the Word Incarnate, and the Holy Spirit have given their names to religious communities.

The divine attributes [18] even the least "communicable" lend their patronage to various modes of spirituality. We find "Adorers of Divine Justice" and "Daughters of Wisdom," both at the service of the unfortunate and the poor. It is because we are reduced—due to the poverty of our vocabulary—to enumerate the Infinite Mercies of our Father that many large communities have taken upon themselves the duty of honoring and serving the unfortunate under many of the attributes "depending on" the divine Goodness. We shall never be able to count all the religious of Providence, of Mercy, and of Charity. The Hotel-Dieu in all countries symbolizes, by its common name, and for all nationalities, the unchangeable goodness of the God of the Christians for all the woes of man. An old institution in Paris has carved deep on its entrance door: "Hospital of Pity."

All the mysteries of the life of Christ, from the manger to the sepulchre, are permanently honored and invoked by the religious of the Holy Child Jesus, the Sacred Heart, the Good Shepherd, the Sisters of the Cross, or the Calvarians.

Our Lady, under this title, without any qualified addition, already dominates tens of Congregations. And we find also, throughout the Church, the Sisters of the Immaculate Conception, the Visitation, the Presentation, of Compassion, of the Cenacle, and of the Assumption. And again there are religious of Our Lady of Mercy, and those of Marie-Auxilia-trice or of Marie-Reparatrice.

Around 1950 when the third centenary of the Foundation of the Sisters of St. Joseph was celebrated, more than sixty Congregations (and some were not represented) had sent delegates from all parts of the world for this great family feast.

One would find it hard to count the religious families sheltered under the patronage of the great patriarchs of the consecrated life in the West alone: Benedictines, Bernardines or Cistercians, Franciscans, and Dominicans.

The Sisters of Saint Vincent de Paul, the second name (and one not less glorious) that the Daughters of Charity bear, are known throughout the world, the true picture of Catholic charity, at the service of every kind of suffering known to man.

It is because these congregations complement one another, and because these services are multiplied and those in charge are anxious to make themselves truly maternal, that we believe in the permanence of religious communities in the Church. They remain irreplaceable in it. Religious of today, like their predecessors, have the confidence of children in their Father Who invites them to follow in their turn the paths which led their elders to perfection and sanctity.

III. OUR COMMON LIFE IN OVERPOPULATED NEIGHBORHOODS

As sincere and very devoted brothers and sisters, we tax our ingenuity in taking our part of the great trial, common to all men. Coexistence is difficult among deafening noises; vulgar brawls among crowded human beings, and almost intolerable sufferings, overwhelm people who are brutalized or exasperated by them. It would not be normal, nor just, that, having the same human nature, religious would not lay claim to their part in sufferings so widespread.

Theoretical definitions tell us that "man is essentially sociable, that is, born to live in a society." [19]

Experience shows us very quickly that sociability is found to be unequally distributed. God had the "dream" of making His children all one family, but original sin has driven that ideal from us. Life, work, and close proximity for the throngs of people in so many countries, have engendered types of suffering scarcely imaginable to those who have never labored with love and interest over the distress of their brethren. From irritation to exasperation, from ill humor to revolt, from complaints to blasphemy, with all the states and shades of difference separating the extremes, each one breathes his complaint or shouts out the excess of his sorrow.

Some facts and some cases

Married couples have sworn to love each other eternally. After some months of living together they find that the reciprocal discovery of defects and limitations is enough to extinguish love, and sometimes even turn it into hatred. Some young people, without ulterior motives, apparently unfitted by discordant natures, make rapid strides in the art of cleverly tormenting one another and in making life mutually intolerable. Both are possessed by the obsession of putting an end to that situation and of escaping from that "slavery."

Two employees can be found who have been for twenty years in the same department or in the same office. Their long-standing mutual antipathy has developed into hatred. Those around them dread scenes.

Our workshops and factories (in spite of great progress

and better conditions) are never completely silent. All their lives crowds of workmen are subjected to the gamut of noises, from nerve-racking irritations to deafening tumults. It is even a harsh trial for the nerves of thousands of employees who must hear, eight hours a day, the rattling of typewriters or calculating machines.

Some of these unfortunates leave this din only to go back to noisy and overcrowded buildings where no single room houses less than two families. How can one be astonished at the inevitability of disputes and quarrels!

Beyond all this distress, there are still more trials to compassionate with. We must mention the sick in hospitals and asylums, the refugees, and displaced persons penned up in their miserable barracks. How can we forget the people in prisons, concentration camps, and jails!

It is true that some ignorant and unthinking people are bored when they are alone. It is possible indeed that some persons have known only life with a group, that of the tent, the clan, and the tribe, and they remain incapable of imagining any other mode of existence. Nevertheless, there has been and will still remain the limitless suffering of those who are exasperated by the appalling certainty that they will never be alone, and that they will die in a room shared by others.

Apostolic utilization of our common life

Starting from these facts, our common life should take on an apostolic meaning. We try to transform its trials so that they can have value in helping our companions in "misery." The knowledge that we have acquired of the goodness and the consideration of our Master authorizes us to represent these things thus.

Our Savior, so compassionate to all human suffering, would not allow a group of afflicted to be devoid of any companions who would lovingly help them bear crushing crosses. When the Lord Himself compares the children of men to the birds of the air, does He not say:

"Are you not worth more than a flight of sparrows?" [20]

We feel therefore that creatures preferred by our Master have the right to priority in our love. The life of our Model, continued among us through His Church, permits it to adapt itself to all varieties as well as all sufferings on this earth. It is one of the manifestations of tenderness of the infinitely loving heart of Jesus to make sure that every trial undergone has its corresponding compensation. Religious, consecrated to Him, therefore, and His friends receive the mission to sanctify the daily and crucified life of their brothers by living it and sharing it.

The common life forms us and aids us in sympathy

The graces of our vocation, although powerful, can never free us from certain natural repugnances which are inevitable in the harsh demands of life in common. Almost all religious of the world agree with the judgment passed by a young saint, canonized especially for his heroic fidelity to the Rule:

"Of all the penances which I have had to endure, the hardest was certainly the common life." [21]

With still more authority, St. Paul stresses the meaning and import, and also the utility of our sorrowful experiences:

"God comforts us in all our afflictions that we also may be able to comfort those who are in any distress by the comfort by which we ourselves are comforted." [22]

Those who dream of assuaging, consoling, or even changing the lot of the unfortunate, ought to commence by becoming specialists in all the branches of destitution. The knowledge of the suffering of men is a knowledge too often badly and poorly mastered. But our life in Community gives us appreciable advantages. Our libraries, on account of our poverty, are not always full of books. But on the contrary there is an unwritten encyclopedia which grows richer every day under the roofs of our humble houses. So many sad confidences, patiently listened to, assure the solid bases of that rarely cultivated specialty—compassion enlivened by love. A feeling aroused by pity, a charity which cannot be quenched because its source is the heart of God Himself, combine their mysterious strength to arouse intuitions and stimulate perceptions. It is thus that adorned by its wealth, guided by its light, religious set forth every day on their appointed rounds where sorrowfully the caravan of the afflicted moves along. And these messengers of the pity and tenderness of God will dress wounds, even if they cannot always hope to heal them.

Broken homes . . . and the common life

We dare to hope that some homes will never be destroyed, due in fact to the merits accumulated by the common life of religious. This is one of the many fruits of the fertility of

our consecrated lives. The profound happiness of thousands
of Christian families rests in large part upon this rock. How
reassured they must feel about the future of their joys!

But there remain numberless and almost universal tragedies among so many divorced persons. Our fidelity, set against
that ocean of bitterness, could seem to be as inefficacious as
it is full of irony. Near such a torrent of hatred, what can the
peace of our lives united in charity do for these victims?
Let us not forget first of all the necessary reparations due
for an offense committed against God. A Father suffers when
He sees His children separated, especially when they have
promised fidelity before the altar of His Son. Often religious,
as we have said before, must become mothers to poor children whose mothers must go out to work during the day.
Again it is these sisters who come to bring aid and support
to young wives, cut off prematurely from affection. Their suffering is sometimes so cruel that they have more than need
of an understanding sympathy. Drawing their goodness from
God, religious become clever enough to bring back again
some aims, some reasons for living to these unfortunates who
tell themselves that they are victims of an absolute defeat.

Those who crave silence, and will never have it

It is the rare religious who has not discovered and enjoyed
the blessings of silence. But there are countless religious
doomed to live out their lives in the midst of noise and clamor.

Teachers know the noisy recreation periods and the joyous shouting of lighthearted youth. There are some among
them who disavow the sympathy which others would offer
them.

Their sisters, the hospital nurses, are aware of a whole scale of cries, among which those of nurseries and maternity wards are not alarming. Moreover, there are the demands of the injured, the complaints of invalids. For many years some sisters have passed their lives in the midst of incoherent cries in asylums, which, due to the new remedies and treatments, have recently been lessened. The continual noises of kitchens must be mentioned, and the still more regular sounds in the modernized laundries and the many workrooms, not forgetting loud conversations between the auxiliary staff and the employed.

The world of the religious, therefore, takes a large share of noises which are monotonous, nerve-racking, fatiguing, and unbearable. How much of real sanctity has been achieved through surroundings which are noisy, loud, clangorous and always devastating to the nerves! This is certainly one more obstacle to be overcome in the eager search for God and for His heavenly peace and silence.

The hubbub of populated cities

Religious who visit the poor and the sick in the workers' areas must pass long hours of the day in the midst of a nerve-racking atmosphere, in a perpetual clamor helped along by calls, screams, and disputes. They know the peace that they will enjoy in the evening on returning to their silent convents. But they look forward as eagerly each morning to returning to a world of tumult and agitation. They are definitely resolved never to desert it, firmly decided to share all the trials of those who think of themselves as their own in calling them "Sisters."

Assistance and contribution of con-
templatives to the milling crowds

Silence, when it is exactly observed, can be very trying.
In the cloisters, which the contemplative never leaves, life
in common can have in itself a lot of difficulties and trials.

One must have availed oneself of it in order to realize
all the spiritual and psychological blessings of silence.[23] The
faithful can scarcely believe to what degree of heroism those
can attain who have promised to keep the absolute silence
imposed by their Rule. A Cistercian told me this example of
which he had been a witness during his lifetime. Two lay
brothers, knowing that they chanted off key, never added
their voices in the "Salve Regina," which in Trappist monasteries musters the whole Community each evening at the
feet of the Blessed Virgin. Then my informant stated: "They
have been there thirty years, and we do not yet know (with
the exception of the Father Abbot) the quality of their
voices."

Another testimony somewhat more recent and gathered
likewise in a Trappist monastery, assures me that perpetual
silence has been a harsh trial for young recruits inasmuch as
it is not a question of silence of things, or what is called the
"silence in acting. . . ." The multiple and ordinary noises of
a common room, where some dozens of religious are engaged
in widely different occupations, can quickly try the patience
of some nervous systems.

And to all this must be added the trying penance of a
common dormitory. Mature religious and the Abbot himself
have their fraternal part in this particularly irritating cross.
In convents of women, the bondage of community dormi-

tories and infirmaries is much more frequently met with than in those of men.

Even an average knowledge of the human being ought to be amply sufficient to demonstrate the psychological and nervous consequences of this form of life on many temperaments. And we must also know that virtue and grace are distributed very imperfectly to fortfiy those who live the common life against the sufferings which it entails for us.

Our truly wise God has His reasons not to spare His friends in any way, and to treat them with a kind of paternal severity. A representative number of spiritual writers teach that even with His friends, favored by particular graces, their Heavenly Friend has been pleased to leave them their limitations and natural defects of which they never seem able to free themselves. The most common reason which these authorities give for this is that these failings make for humility.

Moreover is not this the explanation which St. Paul himself gives of his own mysterious trial:

"And I know such a man . . . who was caught up into paradise and heard secret words that man may not repeat. . . . And lest the greatness of the revelations should puff me up, there was given me a thorn for the flesh, a messenger of Satan to buffet me." [24]

It is certainly not forbidden to suggest that there is a genuine advantage for the world of the cloistered to be forced by the experience of their own jangled nerves to sympathize better with all the suffering that unhappy working and living conditions impose upon men.

To those whose habitual environment is a cause of torture,

the saints seem less far away and more kindly when they come to see their own martyrdom detailed in their own language with touching simplicity:

> "To converse with anyone is worse, for the devel then sends me so offensive a spirit of bad temper that I think I could eat people up, nor can I help myself. I feel that I do something when I keep myself under control; or rather our Lord does so when He holds back with His hand anyone in this state from saying or doing anything that may be hurtful to the neighbor or offensive to God."[25]

God Himself is pleased to draw up the plan of our community lives:

> "For what other nation is there upon earth like thy people Israel, whom God went to deliver and make a people for Himself." [26]

> "I will show thee, O man, what is good, and what the Lord requireth of thee; verily to do judgment and to love mercy, and to walk solicitous with thy God." [27]

> "Take courage, and do diligently, and the Lord will be with you in good things." [28]

[1] Psalms, CXXXII, 1.
[2] Psalms, XXXIII, 9.
[3] Sirach, X, 4.
[4] III Kings, X, 24.

[5] I Peter, V, 2-3.

[6] I Cor., XII, 11.

[7] Hebr., XIII, 17.

[8] I Thess., V, 12.

[9] The construction of the Abbey of Saint Ouen at Rouen continued for 200 years.

[10] The pilgrims of today find it the same as it was in the time of the Saint.

[11] Psalms, XLII, 4.

[12] Baruch, IV, 4. Quoted as a motto to the Book of "Usages and Customs" of the Cistercians.

[13] Exodus, XXXIII, 11.

[14] J. Héduit: Catherine de Francheville, Vannes, 1957, p. 135.

[15] Protagoras (96).

[16] St. Teresa, **Autobiography,** Chap. XXXII.

[17] Psalms, XXIV, 8 and 4-5.

[18] **Dict. de Théol. Cath.:** "Attributs divins" et "Catholicisme." Letouzey, 1952.

[19] See the dictionary.

[20] St. Matthew, X, 31.

[21] St. John Berchmans, S.J.

[22] II Cor., I, 4.

[23] Thomas Merton: **The Silent Life,** New York: Farrar, Cudahy, Straus, 1957.

[24] II Cor., XII, 4 and 7.

[25] St. Teresa, **Autobiography,** Chap. XXX.

[26] I Chron., XVII, 21.

[27] Micheas, VI, 8.

[28] II Chron., XIX, 11.

CHAPTER VI

FRATERNAL CHARITY

> "This is my commandment, that you love one another as I have loved you." [1]

A wonderful history still remains unwritten—that of fraternal charity in our religious families. It would be an impressive manuscript and a superb testimony for our fellowmen to study. If hatred has been powerful throughout the centuries, and if it is still bitter throughout the world, the love and the charity of Christ have had victories that have never been described.

The faithful have the right to know and to appreciate better the moral victories that Christ has accomplished through His Church. His constant appeals to love could not be without echoes.

The ruins of old monasteries and the halls of vast motherhouses keep the secret of our joys. The sounds of our feasts have become hushed. Before our times, thousands of our predecessors have known and received the hundredfold promised by our Master. At an age when, in serenity and impartiality, it is possible for us to compare types of love, we feel that the purity and splendor of ours shows that the most satisfactory human love has nothing that can tempt us to envy.

Since it is impossible to narrate in a few pages the greatness of the past, let us render a double testimony to the victories of fraternal charity in religious communities today. In the midst of a world that is so poor in brotherly love, we know how to make a sincere and joyous love triumph on

—the national level,
—and on the international.

I. FRATERNAL CHARITY ON THE NATIONAL LEVEL

There is a fact that can easily be verified in the majority of churches throughout the Catholic world. It is thus:—souls awaken to fraternal charity only with extreme slowness. Parishes in every country have still much to do to make their faithful *brothers* in the Christian and evangelical meaning of the word.

Traditions, customs, prejudices, and deep feelings divide persons into many classes. Positions, trades, professions, social conventions, political passions, and above all, money, dig trenches or abysses which isolate and separate people into opposing castes or parties. The really poor have difficulty in believing and feeling themselves brothers of the rich. Too many deeds, words, and reflections, even simple but uncontrollable reflexes, of the wealthy humiliate them painfully.

Liberation and exorcism of religious life

It is from this mold that religious life liberates us; it frees us from all these prejudices by exorcising them. This is one of the first victories and advantages of fraternal charity.

Our Mother the Church is proud of the fact that she has encouraged the great orders and congregations to seek recruits in all social classes. In these groups that are truly families, new hierarchies can be established in simplicity and reciprocal confidence. Virtue, good qualities and gifts alone determine position, employment, or function. It is not rare to find that the children of workmen or of servants have become the competent major superiors of the daughters of financial leaders or the heiresses of great and ancient families. Experience proves that this does not hinder in any way the relations between them. Religious succeed in forgetting what in too worldly a language is called "humble extraction." True virtue and the gifts of God enrich and ennoble souls so much that total and blind confidence is given to these guides.

Progressive stages in this liberation

In the novitiate

We instinctively love the persons who give us in large measure the God Who dwells within them. When we have had the privilege of benefiting for months from filial relations with a beloved mother, we cannot forget the important dates that mark our climb up the mountain of perfection. There are words which seem to come from the very heart of God; there are appeals so precise and urgent that they mark, overturn, and transform our lives. Paths are smoothed and horizons widened. We breathe another air and penetrate into an entirely new world. How many young disciples can repeat what so many of their elders have said:

> "Now we have received not the spirit of the world, but the spirit that is from God, that we may know the things that have been given us by God." [2]

Atmosphere of sisterliness

Ignorance of the past history of individuals favors the possibility of deep and fruitful friendships. The daughters of bitter competitors or of irreconcilable political enemies may draw profit, simply and without any ulterior motive, from the human affinity that draws them together. Their Master has endowed them so that they may work in fruitful collaboration.

In such a friendly and kindly atmosphere, many persons will reveal their real capabilities. If they are by nature diffident and timid, a sceptical or jealous atmosphere would have sterilized their good will, or perhaps the situation and poverty of their family would have made them feel insignificant. Encouraged and sustained by this universal confidence, their human personality, which sometimes is very rich, will profit a whole community. God, in His fatherly love, constantly enriches religious communities with these persons who have been transformed by love.

To appreciate its benefits, we must have experienced all the consequences of this liberation. How many good qualities make possible the victories over selfishness, foolish vanity, lack of simplicity, and the paralyzing desire to wound or dominate humiliated rivals. Having regained a child-like ingenuousness, we put in the service of everyone the gifts received from God for the joy and advantage of others.

The assimilation wrought by fraternal charity

Twenty centuries after St. Paul, there are in our religious communities loving guides who make their own the prayer of the great Apostle whose spirit is still living in the Church,

"For God is my witness how I long for you all in the heart of Christ Jesus. And this I pray that your charity may more and more abound in knowledge and all discernment, so that you may approve the better things, that you may be upright and without offense unto the day of Christ, filled with the fruit of justice, through Jesus Christ, to the glory and praise of God." [3]

It is only after contemplating it for a long time that we believe in the moral splendor that shines forth in the groups of persons who have been freed from prejudice; they are the privileged children of the Father Who is love. The victories won in analogous domains by all those pioneers of charity lead them to the evangelic virtue stated clearly by St. John,

"By this will all men know that you are my disciples, if you have love one for another." [4]

What we love with an ever-growing love in those around us are the victories charity has won in liberating their souls. How can we doubt that God makes our community one of His temples where He delights to dwell? This permanent presence of the Trinity in our hearts sheds around us dazzling light.

"He who loves his brother abides in the light." [5]

"Beloved, let us love one another, for love is from God. And everyone who loves is born of God, and knows God." [6]

From the happy moment that charity has led us to these heights, we share in the benevolence that the Lord bestows upon His creatures. The Most High associates us in His pity and His kindness that is full of tenderness; and also in that joy of which He is the inexhaustible source. He gives this as an enviable hundredfold to all those who, in order to follow His Son, have sacrificed voluntarily but often with heart-breaking sorrow, all the human happiness offered them.

Tender charity for our companions in difficulties

It is a well-known fact that religious are ordinarily recruited from large families. The number of our brothers and sisters has brought us many joys, and each year renews happy anniversaries. But a sizeable family multiplies the risks of trials and sorrows. We do not usually consider the number of those letters that converge upon monasteries and convents, bearing heart-rending secrets. Mothers who are humiliated by the dearest of their children, brothers and sisters who no longer speak to one another, having quarreled over some inheritance, or who are jealous and spiteful when they are not all equally successful; all these turn towards the religious whom they consider "the angel of the family," and whom "the victims," "the oppressed," "the sacrificed" take as their advocate.

If charity develops and transforms so many of these religious, it leaves intact their affection for their families, and sometimes it increases it a hundredfold. Having often experienced other troubles, their sensibility tortures them when they receive certain letters from their dear ones. They read them with tears in their eyes. It is on such occasions that fraternal charity knows how to be ingenious and tactful.

The best qualified interpreters of our Lord, the two great souls chosen by Love, were St. John the Evangelist and St. Paul. We believe and feel with them when they tell us that the charity which comes to us from the very heart of God enlightens us in every way. It is, therefore, capable of enriching us with all the gifts of psychology, strengthening our intuitions and discernment. Then with awareness and tact one finds the exact words which, being suitable, do not wound the sensibilities of an afflicted companion; thus his suffering will be lessened.

Fraternal charity, source and guarantee of our joys

Many religious are ignorant of Dante's wonderful command, but they would not have as much trouble as others in fulfilling it. "Having come forth from a joyful Creator, let us instinctively run towards joy." [7]

The Creator of joy leads us toward it. From our first steps in the religious house that accepted us, joy came upon us and has remained faithful to us. St. Teresa tells us:

"When I took the habit our Lord at once made me understand how He helps those who do violence to themselves in order to serve Him. . . . At that moment, because I was entering on that state, I was filled with a joy so great that it has never failed me to this day." [8]

St. Bernadette felt the same kind of joy on the day of her profession. But when one recalls the eighteen apparitions at the Grotto of Lourdes, the expression of the happiness of the new religious appears even more striking, "I believed myself in Heaven."

Two great religious and two great saints speak the same language. The celebrated Prioress of St. Joseph of Avila does not hesitate to sum up her experience in giving us this description of her poor and humble Carmel:

> "In the measure that there can be a Heaven on earth, this Heaven is under our roof." [9]

If the best of our joys are of heavenly origin, they appear in very human forms. Let us not forget that very ancient texts, in recommending virtues and good qualities to our distant predecessors in the faith, did not omit "lightness" [10] which is still defined as gentle and habitual gaiety. We keep this tradition as a family treasure.

We have our feast days, our days of profession and the jubilees that recall them. The feast or anniversary of the superior practically becomes the feast of the Community. We celebrate the departure and arrival of our missionaries; the receiving of university degrees, of nurses' diplomas, individual or collective distinctions are all stressed . . . the range of joy is often great.

In this domain, examples as well as recommendations often come from the orders that are reputed the most austere. The note of joy, introduced by the Reformer of Carmel into her very first monasteries, has been transmitted intact through four centuries. One of the most recent editions of her *Foundations* [11] is accompanied by photographic documents among which is one that proves to us that "dancing was not banished from all cloisters."

St. Teresa knew how to set the tradition, which she established, upon her personal example. In her correspondence we find this delightful note:

"I have nothing to send you today but my songs (according to the context, it was not a question of hymns) which my confessor had me compose for the joy of my Sisters. The air to them is pleasing and easily learned."

St. John Bosco, the beloved father of hundreds of orphans, was a joyous saint. A witness has told me this: When in 1883 the Founder of the Salesians came to Paris, his reputation as a wonder-worker had preceded him there. The majority of Catholics of this period still associated their conception of sanctity with evident austerity. The "pilgrims" who had visited Ars were still numerous. They had not forgotten the heavenly smile of the holy Cure, but they had been even more struck by his extraordinary seriousness. This time they were "offered" only a jovial Italian who enjoyed life. The disappointment they felt was almost general.

The Church, an incomparable Teacher, in order to increase and strengthen our confidence in the lovable guides who lead us to joy, instructs us by her liturgy. For a long time, the Carmelite missals had a special Mass for the feast of St. Teresa on October 15. Its introit was particularly striking. Now it is this truly lyric text that the Church offers her faithful on January 31, feast of St. John Bosco.

"And God gave him wisdom and understanding exceeding much, and largeness of heart as the sand that is on the seashore." [12]

It is from such hearts, the greatest of human hearts, that we receive instructions for our fraternal joy. As a kind and understanding mother, the Church, faithfully interpreting the thought and will of God, does not hesitate to recommend joy to us now as she did at the dawn of her history. She invites us to study the teaching of the surest masters in the science of our vocation.

II. OUR FRATERNAL CHARITY ON THE INTERNATIONAL LEVEL

"They will come from the east and from the west, from the north and from the south, and will feast in the kingdom of God." [13]

Every morning in certain motherhouses sisters who belong to every nation represented at the U.N. receive Communion side by side. Throughout the months they make progress towards a more complete understanding of one another; they mutually enrich one another with the treasures of their races and of their past. To be able to view these marvels at close range is a remarkable grace from God. It quickly persuades one that such a union can be brought about only in love.

"Whether Jews or Gentiles, whether slaves or free . . . we were all given to drink of one Spirit." [14]

St. Paul limits his enumeration to the races and conditions of the first Chirstian era. The Gospel has now been preached to all the nations assembled in our day in great international organizations. The priest who, in passing down the long Communion rail sees on communicants' faces the whole gamut of colors, feels almost that there has been a miracle worked by love.

"Knowing that their Lord who is also your Lord is in heaven, and with him there is no respect of persons." [15]

Just as the Lord has no respect for persons, He has none for categories and divisions made by man. Being the Creator of all, He loves them all with the same fatherly love. His benevolence does not exclude or reject any human group.

"Your Father in heaven, Who makes His sun rise on the good and the evil, and sends rain on the just and the unjust." [16]

Our universal Father bears the same interest for wandering tribes and despised clans. After twenty centuries of preaching, Christ has now offered the practice of the evangelical counsels to the children of all the races on the face of the earth. If some isolated peoples, such as the Kurds or the gypsies, "the Children of the Road and of the Wind," [17] have not yet been called, apostolates are preparing in these groups the first fruits of tomorrow's vocations.[18]

A message that all can assimilate

Because it comes from a Father, the message can be assimilated by all. Nothing can be an obstacle to it, no civilization or culture, no past, no form of thought. The least among the children of men is capable of participating in the nobility of God. Historians of civilizations and psychologists could be amazed that persons, marked by the atavism of races or castes, by mentalities and prejudices, could attain a common manner of understanding poverty, chastity, obedience, humility, and fraternal charity. When one has had the privilege of being invited "to read souls," those sanctuaries where complete sincerity is formed and developed, one cannot but extol the power of God over the hearts of men. He takes in His hands the hearts of His chosen ones and imprints on them the seal of fraternal love. It becomes impossible to doubt that the soul has been made to the image of God. It matters little of what material the mirrors are made; they all receive the faithful reflection of God's beauty.

No devastating uniformity

In all fields and in all countries when it prospers, Catholicity respects all the differences due to race, civilization, and history, as well as to the mentality and habits of so many Catholics united in the same Church.

As children sharing the views of their beloved Mother, the most fervent and saintly religious do not ignore the fact that they have the duty, the right, and the need of always loving their country and their race, of associating themselves with their joys, sharing their trials, and weeping over their sorrows.[19] If anyone has lived for years in large cosmopolitan communities, he knows and admires the way the national feasts of all the peoples of the earth are joyfully celebrated in a fraternal spirit. It is a way of participating anew in the love of God, in that fondness and interest which, as an impartial Father, He has for all the countries peopled by His children.

The common treasury to which all contribute

Much complementary wealth, brought from all the continents, is incarnate in the varied members of our large communities; for this reason we feel that we benefit from the hundredfold promised by God. For years we live under the same roof in an intimacy such as only religious life provides. It is therefore possible for us to learn and understand many things, to grasp and appreciate many points of view, to enrich ourselves with details and nuances that only citizens of a well-loved country are capable of explaining to us. People have difficulty to imagine the extraordinary advantage there can be in counting brethren and friends in more than fifty countries.

Compassion extended to the measure of the world

When religious have become truly fraternal in heart, they succeed in making their own the sadness and distress suffered by those whom they tenderly love.

An expert in charity, seeing sadness on another's face or melancholy in her glance, perceives that she is homesick. The grey skies of a northern country are very depressing for those who come from countries of dazzling light. When one has seen for years only cloudless skies, it is a hard trial to see the sun only rarely. It is then that another sister can draw forth enchanting descriptions of countries she will never visit but whose beauties she can divine from the enthusiastic accounts given by those who dearly love their native land.

But there is a sadness that is more profound and more difficult to dispel. Knowing this, those with compassionate hearts provide themselves with information and sympathy as wide as the expanse of continents. They know how to listen to harrowing testimony on the poverty of under-developed countries or on the fratricidal wars kept up by age-old hatreds. They succeed in sincerely making their own the sorrow of a humble sister who is the daughter of an African or Brazilian tribe. Oh! how kind and sisterly are those religious who have become the studious disciples of Sirach or of St. Paul. Since misery pursues all generations, the pity of God expresses the same counsels after the interval of centuries.

"Avoid not those who weep, but mourn with those who mourn." [20]

"Weep with those who weep." [21]

In the school of the greatest teachers,
God and the Church

As members of large Catholic communities, religious feel their love for the Church is increased and strengthened. They are in a position to view at close range the successes of this Mother. They see to what extent her confidence is rewarded. Sisters whose parents were still pagan have become the fervent rivals of the descendants of almost fifty generations of Christians. Religious witness with admiration the advance of the Kingdom of God throughout the world. Some of their humble and fervent companions are like the ambassadors of their people. Their vocation has flourished through the fidelity of a group of truly Christian families surrounded by masses of indifferent people who are materialistic or pagan. In spite of apparent set-backs and of the persecutions that she has always known, the Church is always increasing in souls whom she arouses to the ideals of the Gospel.

God knows how to utilize, as no one else can, the qualities

of all peoples and all races. The limitless devotion, the tenacity in working, the conscientiousness and fidelity of Oriental religious are the transformation of the natural qualities of the Chinese coolies, Javanese planters, and the rice gatherers of Madagascar. God proves to us that every human soul whom He has chosen can rise to true holiness; and this no matter what may be the past history of her race and the slowness of her people's ascent towards the light. Wise men may speak of the weight of heredity. Infinite Wisdom shows us that His grace is sovereign. As trustful children of this universal Father, we open the ranks of our communities in welcome to all His chosen ones. We end by sharing in the very benignity of God, concurring with blind confidence to the view of Him Who has the transcendent advantage of reading the depths of hearts.

"Hear thou from heaven, from thy high dwelling place, and forgive and render to everyone according to his ways which thou knowest him to have in his heart (for thou only knowest the hearts of the children of men) . . .

"If the stranger also who is not of thy people Israel, come from a far country, for the sake of thy great name . . . hear thou from heaven, thy firm dwelling place, and do all that which the stranger shall call upon thee for; that all people of the earth may know thy name." [22]

Advantages for our apostolates

On the apostolic plane, this cosmopolitanism is beneficial and irreplaceable. The apostle needs to know always better the human soul. Now, we are capable of discovering an extraordinary brotherhood among the souls of all men. It matters little what is their appearance or their country. God reserves for them the same welcome; He adorns His chosen souls with the same gifts.

In our large communities, we can verify the fact that among all it is "the same soul" that is climbing the mount of perfection. Our Father offers holiness to all, and in His generosity, He makes greatness and heroism possible for the children of all races. We would be capable of furnishing endless testimony to this fact. Without ever leaving their country, religious do not have far to seek in the Lord's immense field for the evidence of His power to transfigure souls. In the community where their life is passed, they see companions coming to them from the four corners of the world; these are already adorned with solid virtues that permit them to become their equals in the ascent towards God.

Our charity is ceaselessly widened and improved

To love God and to be loved by Him works ideal transformations in souls. Divine Love progressively models our love on His. Ours is joined to that of our Guide in regard to all the beings He loves and invites us to love.

> "From the moment that God enkindles in our hearts the fire of His love, we begin to love, not only the One Who is love, but all beings, all souls loved by our Father, the guide and model of our love." [23]

It is to our affectionate care that the Master of the world

has confided the treatment which He has "dreamed" for His privileged souls. If they had remained in their own environment, some would have had difficulty in finding the tactful consideration their great Friend had destined for them. Who would have protected them against the attitudes and simple reflexes caused in others by the instinctive feelings, scorn and contempt from which an ordinary grace does not free all souls.

Many experience a great difficulty in triumphing over appearances, those envelopes that veil true moral beauty.

When one yields to the liberating truth that all souls have a Divine origin, charity has won the last and most difficult of its victories. Those sent by the Lord have furnished the other half of the road. They have benefited notably by being freed from prejudices. At a time when there is so little brotherly feeling between races, it is too often forgotten that if a religious of one nationality feels aversion or repugnance in regard to her sisters belonging to another, the latter feel against her a no less violent repugnance.

Now, without any merit on their part, religious meet on the elevated plane of charity. The strong current of charity has purified the atmosphere even in the middle of the twentieth century when one of the greatest dramas of mankind is being enacted—the universal revolt of the colored races against the white. Religious belonging to all nations and tribes on the surface of the globe live together in peace and happiness. This is one of the most brilliant and successful results of fraternal charity. Many of the faithful have the right and the need of knowing that among religious, obstacles have been surmounted and almost all victories have been won. The charity of God triumphs in all its splendor.

Facts and testimony

At the present moment all the Christian countries profit by our great fraternal assemblies. By generous exchanges, Congregations of religious women circulate throughout the world the descendants of all nations. Above all let us thank the Church who has inspired such a sense of catholicity in the best of her children. A sister of no matter what country can benefit with her devotedness and apostolate persons of all nations. She understands so well that every man is a child of God that she loves and serves him, surrounding him with a charity without reserve as well as without self-interest.

In certain cases a religious will be particularly happy to devote herself to the compatriots of the apostle who had come a great distance to reveal to her what true charity is. Since they keep their human affections, religious can suffer even heartbreak on leaving forever their beloved country. In her mission school or leprosarium, it is a consolation for such an exile to know that one of her sisters of a different country, who made the same sacrifice as she did, is now replacing her in the service of the children, the old, and the poor of her own race, all of whom she had once dreamed of helping personally.

Invited to the banquet presided over by God Himself and under His fatherly glance, we have gathered together from all countries and from all horizons. We no longer speak a language that is too earthly. Feeling that we are the children of the same Father with the same claims and identical rights, we believe in only one hierarchy, that of love.

We are already in the antechamber of Heaven, enlightened by the rays that filter through the gates. We know that "the city has no need of the sun or the moon to shine on it for the glory of God lights it up, and the Lamb is the lamp thereof." [24]

We are comprised of peoples and tribes far surpassing in number the twelve tribes of Israel. To those who can understand, God presents us as the pioneers of "a great multitude which no man can number, out of all nations and tribes and peoples and tongues." [25]

Forming this privileged vanguard and conscious of the predilection of our Father and Friend, we pray that brothers and sisters will come to us from all human families and even from those wandering tribes which, despised by many, have not yet given the best of their children to our religious groups where a most fraternal love is promised them.[26]

[1] John, XV, 12.

[2] I Corinthians, II, 12.

[3] Philippians, I, 8-10.

[4] St. John, XIII, 35.

[5] I St. John, II, 10.

[6] I St. John, IV, 7.

[7] Light intellectual, replete with love; Love of true happiness, replete with joy; Joy, that transcends all sweetness of delight. (The Divine Comedy: Paradise, Canto XXX.)

[8] Life, Chapter IV.

[9] The Way of Perfection, Chapter XIV.

[10] Dictionnaire d'Archeologie et de Liturgie, "Catéchèse," 2, 552.

[11] That of Marcelle Auclair.

[12] III Kings, IV, 29.

[13] St. Luke, XIII, 29.

[14] I Corinthians, XIII, 13.

[15] Ephesians, VI, 9.

[16] St. Matthew, V, 45.

17 They were so called by the great poet, Tzigane Tikno Adjam who died in 1948.

18 Missi, April, 1959: Gypsies, eternal wanderers.

19 Cry, Beloved Country.

20 Sirach, VII, 34.

21 Romans, XII, 15.

22 II Paralipomenon, VI, 30-33.

23 St. Leo.

24 Apocalypse, XXI, 23.

25 Ibid., VII, 9. Cf. Documentation Catholique, July 5, 1959, col. 864. Count dalla Torre: Osservatore Romano, June 17, 1959.

26 Even while writing this, we see on the hill above us the College of the Propaganda where all races and all colors are united, a living rainbow, a sign of peace, and an invitation to peace extended to all men of good will.

CHAPTER VII

PRAYER

"And you shall call upon me . . . and you shall pray to me, and I will hear you." [1]

The greatest of religious, our most loved and surest guides, have taken their places among the "pioneers" of prayer. The intimate union which they have had with God carried them forward to light and sanctity. Placing ourselves under their instruction and following in their footsteps, we have the well-grounded hope of gaining, among other advantages, a double benefit from our prayer:

It will be enlightened
It will become fruitful.

I. PRAYER: THE SOURCE OF LIGHT

The Saints are the explorers of God. Their prayer has conducted them to the world of light. We are invited to join them, and following them, to draw profit from the great discoveries to which God makes Himself the infallible guide. Some pioneers have preceded us and advanced so far into the depths of Infinite Truth that they are, as it were, beacon lights for souls on the way to the Source of all knowledge.

The Saints have drawn maps of their explorations and left us their accounts in most surprising pages.

Our predecessors in the religious life: St. Benedict and St. Bernard, St. Bonaventure and St. Thomas Aquinas, St. Ignatius of Loyola and St. Teresa of Avila, St. John of the Cross as well as St. Alphonsus Liguori or St. Grignon de Montfort remain our great teachers, and ones always to be listened to.

When minds have had their fill of drinking from "broken cisterns" they turn toward "the fountains of living water." [2] And then it is that they begin their real advance toward the Light.

On the transcendence of God

Beginning with a reassuring intuition one can arrange his life according to the hierarchy of values.

"For I am thy God, and there is no other." [3]

"That they may know . . . from the rising of the sun to its setting . . . that there is none beside me, and all else is vanity." [4]

One arrives at a point where he can no longer think of anything else but that God would be the "First to be served." That confers a spirit, inculcates an enduring way of thinking. One has at last come to the blessed inability of imagining any other order of things. A way of living has been discovered, and this is the first fruit of Prayer, the source of light.

Hunger and thirst for truth

God is the Ocean of all truth. Prayer quickens in our hearts an insatiable need for light. To our advantage the encouraging promises of the Holy Scriptures are realized:

> "We shall know, and we shall follow on, that we may know the Lord. His going forth is prepared as the morning light, and he will come to us as the early and latter rain to the earth." [5]

We bear in our hearts the certainty of rapid progressions toward the transfiguring divine light. God has made us understand that it is He Himself who awakens our desires, who initiates our longings.

> "Behold the days come, saith the Lord, and I will send forth a famine into the land; not a famine of bread, nor a thirst of water, but of hearing of the word of God. . . . They shall go about seeking the word of God, and shall not find it." [6]

It is enough to have practiced assiduous, patient, and faithful prayer in order to experience the profound knowledge of God that such attention and filial pursuit can bring. And it is often in times of prayer that reading we have done, or explanations we have listened to, come together in excellent syntheses. When God arouses the craving, and the need for truth, He reserves to Himself the filling of the void which He has deepened; He answers expectations aroused without disappointing them.

Interior light dispels darkness

There are other domains in which prayer becomes enlightening. God dwells in souls. Therefore He is the best and surest guide to explore the hearts of men. Sincere suppliants beg God to precede them in the very difficult probing of their own interior. It was the beginning of a blessed day when God cast the beam of His pitiless light over the deeply hidden folds of our hearts, on darkness sometimes complacently retained, so that our religious lives could be transformed.

"O my people, pour out your hearts before Him." [7]

"The eyes of the Lord, ten thousand times brighter than the sun, observe every step a man takes and peer into hidden corners . . . a ray emanating from Him makes the darkest shadows luminous and dazzling." [8]

Prayer facilitates exploration into the beauty of souls

"We see now through a glass in a dark manner but then face to face. Now I know in part, but then I shall know even as I am known." [9]

Between the enigmas of life here below and the Beatific Vision, there are many intermediate stages. Illuminating prayer will aid us in going forward through them. It teaches us some of the laws operating in the world of souls.

It carries us far away from those regions where material things, the body, affluence, and only physical beauty triumph. Prayer opens to us another world than that in which the order of importance ranges from comfort to material inventions or successful techniques. Prayer shows us superb and profound souls in malformed bodies, among incurable invalids, faithful images of Christ Who has already welcomed them into His Kingdom. Passions are overcome, rancor done away with, and enemies are loved. We realize in amazement to what depth this sincerity can go, and to what a height ideal and moral beauty can rise. We admire the charity and the virtues of those who seek God. We learn to compassionate with their regrets, their sorrows, and their disappointment at the slowness and the difficulty of their spiritual ascension.

New discoveries concerning other laws of divine pedagogy

There are aspects and gradations of the tenderness of God that one must have enjoyed in order to measure its depth.

"How great is the goodness, O Lord, which you have in store for those who fear you. . . . You hide them in the shelter of your presence. You screen them within your abode." [10]

What a favor to feel oneself moving smoothly along on that ocean of goodness; what discoveries are there for the voyagers on that limitless sea! We know that God wishes many souls to enjoy these experiences, created as they are to His own image, and invited to His feast of love. We have the feeling that this wonderful Friend seeks to multiply the messengers of His kindness. He issues His orders in peaceful form:

"For His anger lasts but a moment, His good will, a lifetime." [11]

Those intimate with God, by dint of studying His "style" and His manner of being, are enlightened about the "preoccupations" and what one might call the "obsessions" of the Father, and recognize an inward duty to rally all to His wishes. Religious cannot forget that superiors are to them "Vicars of God," and therefore the best qualified interpreters of the divine Will. Freely submitting then to the decisions of obedience, suppliants begin by seeing, during the hours of their contact with God, the order of immediacy and the priority of duties to be undertaken. With the light that clarifies, those who pray respect instinctively all the preferences and predilections of God. They know that they cannot ask an accounting of Him. Why did the Lord prefer Jacob to Esau?

"O man, who art thou to reply to God? . . . Is not the potter master of his clay to make from it what seems good to him?" [12]

Rallying to that unquestionable principle, the habitues of prayer accept the choice made by their Father of a step on the new Jacob's ladder [13] where He has placed them in the immense hierarchy of suppliants. They know that Heaven has its terrestrial counterpart and that here below there are "many mansions of the Father's house." [14] Very happy to have been welcomed into one of them, religious given to prayer try to respond to all the appeals of their Master. They are fully aware not only that the ascents are possible, but that they are offered. And since they know how good the

Lord is, they try not to show themselves too unworthy to be raised up to the "mansions" of which the saintly Prioress of Carmel recounts the beauties in her *Interior Castle*.

Souls of prayer know all the revelations to which the gift of contemplation can lead them. They can then run on without stopping, and that prayer becomes ever more enlightening:

> ". . . But very often our Lord will not give to some the grace of contemplation in twenty years while He gives it to others in one. His Majesty knoweth why. . . . In this matter our Lord imparts perhaps a deeper knowledge to some illiterate old woman than to (a director) although he may be a very learned man." [15]

Nothing can resist the "drive" of this light. A religious could even specify the day and the minute when he felt himself exorcised of the exaggerated patriotism which had possessed him until that time. Again, when someone had done him a considerable injury, humanly exasperating, he begged God to give him the strength to pardon it. His Master made him understand that He was drying up the springs of hatred and ill-will in his heart. Some decades have gone by since then, but the divine promises were kept, inasmuch as they remained constantly efficacious.

II. FRUITFULNESS OF THE PRAYER OF RELIGIOUS

Pope Pius XI spoke one time of the "all-powerful prayer of little children." Because so many religious have regained their childlike hearts they can make their prayers share in the irresistible power of praise and supplication of the little ones.

In the numerous domains where the fruitfulness of prayer can be used let us rapidly review three worlds: those of praise, consecration, and supplication.

1. *The prayer of praise*

If the history of the praise chanted by our predecessors, like that of our fraternal charity, still remains to be written, the essentials and documents of that history have not all disappeared. Often enough, in surroundings made illustrious throughout a long past, present-day suppliants could constantly improve their understanding of the grandeur and beauty of God. They have received from their elders throughout the centuries a permanent lesson of praise, that which teaches the primacy of what is divine, what is sacred, and what is of absolute preference. . . .

Religious never cease in all climes and at all the canonical hours to repeat that God is great, that He is good, powerful, just, beautiful and rich in mercy. Candles and incense become the speaking symbols of their consecrated lives. They are entirely consumed and their vapors rise to Heaven to glorify God, just as there are generations of monks and nuns who have spent their lives in praise. I have it from one of the historians of the Carthusian Order [16] that at the most flourishing era of their history, the Carthusians had 300 monasteries in Europe. The glory that the contemplatives celebrate, and the praise that goes on from sunrise to sunset, and even during the night, all ascends towards the throne of the Eternal God and glorifies Him forever.

As soon as the singers leave the stalls of their age-old choirs, they regroup around

"the four and twenty ancients, clothed in white garments, and on their heads crowns of gold." [17]

Their loving and permanent role is to gather and assemble all the praises uttered by terrestrial voices in order to transmit them, magnified and redolent of love, to the Sovereign Master.

"Know, therefore, that when you prayed, you and Sara, it was I (Raphael) who offered your prayers to the Lord Who heard them." [18]

Terrestrial Praise

Before being offered to God, the praise which rises from earth must be collected and then assembled. When one understands praise, then he desires it to be as full and complete as possible. Contemplatives know how to survey creation in order to obtain from it the full amount of glory which they can express through it. In their silent walks, the monks of Monte Cassino, those of Assisi, of the Grand Chartreuse, and of Montserrat look at the vast horizons or the austere surroundings in order to celebrate still better the glory of the Creator. Then from these remote horizons they bring back their attention to the humble blade of grass, the insect, or the sparrow.

Far beyond the visible and material world, there is the kingdom of souls and hearts. Without exploring it, like apostles, contemplatives know that it is in that universe of minds

that they will find the rudiments of glory praising God, the
Friend of men. We cannot easily trace the mysterious ways
uniting cottages and palaces, schools and factories, hospitals
as well as the prisons with monasteries or abbeys. It is through
these ways that desires and dreams come, and with them the
ideal, great honesty and heroism, as well as the joy of grateful souls or the indescribable sufferings of broken hearts.
This is the time to recall the question of a monk of our times:

"Why cannot prayer send forth waves like light and the
sun?" [19]

If our monasteries can "broadcast" they can also be "recep-
tors." It is therefore to these heights of praise that all continents could send discordant chants or inexpert praises to be
harmonized there.

Other classes of souls and persons must not be neglected
or forgotten. In the very heart of the masses, we could not
count the number of ignorant or careless—all to whom negligence has become a habit and a condition. God would never
be thanked or praised by them if the contemplatives, devoted
to praise, did not offer it in their name and in their place.
Too heedless to suspect it, entire nations find interpreters
who thank God and praise Him for having created them. For
such things as health, strength, and material goods lavished
on them by a generous Father, unceasing thanksgiving is
sent up to Heaven.

2. Prayer of Consecration

New questions are put to the present-day singers of the
glory of God. This, for example: in order to be more effica-

cious and more competent, would not prayer gain by being better informed? For centuries, contemplatives have sincerely and truly glorified God even though they knew practically nothing of the nature of things. But the "consecrators" of the beauty of the world, of the power and the marvels of matter, have no longer the right to ignore the immense and unremitting labor expended by researchers in every country. Thanks to these pioneers, we have begun to discover some of the secrets of the human body, and to penetrate more deeply into those of life itself. Diseases are overcome, one after another.

It is now permsisible to speak of "dramas of praise." Scientists complain with evident sadness of the total ignorance, even the disdain, shown by the majority of people concerning the problems to which they devote themselves. The professionals of prayer, almost without exception, if they cannot be accused of disdain and contempt for their learned brothers, ought to have the humility and simplicity to admit that in large part they deserve the reproach that follows:

> "I am often in consternation at the incredible unawareness of the most rudimentary facts concerning (the science I am pursuing) displayed by my comrades, the historians, or by statesmen I know, or among my acquaintances or my friends, the business men. They have no idea what is going on in physics at the present time. And I firmly believe that they have no notion of what is being done in any scientific set up." [20]

On the other hand, let us guard against another part of the discouraging demands, and acknowledge that our most guileless religious, least expert in human knowledge, have remembered to thank God "Who has given such power to men." [21]

Let us still believe in the superiority of love over all other orders. In the face of the infinite knowledge of God, our giants of scientific discovery are nothing more than pygmies. They will never be anything but poor if they have no love. On returning from their observatories or laboratories, if they are human at all, they can quickly re-adapt themselves to simple language, to the meagre vocabulary of their youngest children. They should therefore understand that simple souls, but very loving ones, keep their way of speaking to their Heavenly Father of all the marvels of His creation.

It is not out of place to mention here that a man of prayer, who was neither an astronomer nor a mathematician, had the filial habit of offering to God each morning the homage of a galaxy, numbering billions of stars.

The most recent of our "consecrations"

Those engaged permanently in prayer remain human enough to be on the watch for the latest advances in science. The refinement of their love for God has provided them with harmonious reflexes. At the exact moment when they hear a new discovery spoken of, and even before they express admiration at the success of their brothers, they send up to God thanks and homage.

The exact and complete history of praise can be written only in the Book of God. But we must not hesitate to believe that it is in our religious families that we must seek for those loving souls who merit the enviable title of "pioneers of Praise." From their hearts goes to God the first "Thank You"

from the earth for a scientific triumph, or the success of a
new operation.

This kind of priority would suffice to illustrate the whole
life of a man of prayer. Thus, in the unthinking crowd, we
lead our marvelous lives of privileged children. Sublimity is
often shown by contrast. Some religious are so unpretentious
that the city or town which shelters them is unaware of their
existence, but they fill one of the most enviable roles: offering homage and returning thanks to God for the power He
has given to men.

3.   Prayer of Supplication

The profession of Advocate is one of the finest occupations of men. It becomes a sublime one when a petitioner,
kneeling before God, tries to defend one of his brothers. God
is so good that from the most distant times, He has deigned
to talk with man for the benefit of the guilty.

Moses did not fear to brave the anger of the Eternal God.
He pleaded fearlessly the cause of the builders of the Golden
Calf:

> "Let your blazing wrath die down; relent in punishing
> your people. Remember your servants, Abraham, Isaac,
> and Jacob! . . . And the Lord relented in the punishment
> He had threatened to inflict on His people." [22]

One of the early friends of God discovered His "weakness." He touches upon it therefore, in recalling to the mind
of the Father, His children, His just men, and His handiwork.

> "But You, O almighty One, have mercy on all. . . . For

You love all things that are made and loathe nothing which You have made." [23]

That Heavenly Father is not demanding about the number of just necessary to save a city. If fifty cannot be found, He will be content with ten.[24]

In order to encourage the petitioners of all times, there are texts condensing for us His unwearying pursuit, and His search for His chosen but unfaithful people.

"And Thou didst forbear with them for many years, and didst testify against them by Thy spirit by the hands of Thy prophets. . . ." [25]

Why should we not remain full of confidence in our fraternal pleas, when we surprise God in conversation with one of the prophets? It is He Who takes in hand the cause of mercy and defends it, putting into it all the love of a Father. Jonas finishes by crying out, full of vexation:

"Ah! I know that Thou art a gracious and merciful God, patient and of much compassion, and easy to forgive evil." [26]

The Lord now lays before the eyes of His adversary the touching reason for His forgiveness:

"Thou art grieved for the ivy which thou hast not fostered nor made it grow, and which in one night came up and in one night perished. And shall not I spare Ninive, that great city, in which there are more than one hundred and twenty thousand persons that know not how to distinguish their right hands from their left, and many beasts?" [27]

There are still avengers of the rights of God like those who range from Jonas to the two sons of Zebedee, the "sons of Thunder," [28] or as they are often described, "fulminators and destroyers." [29]

It is striking to see how God, our Lord, and the Blessed Virgin, Mother of Mercy and the Refuge of Sinners, have been careful to answer them. It was on behalf of a people, guilty, like so many others, that Our Lady of Pontmain said to four village children on January 17, 1871: "Pray, my children, that my Son will allow Himself to be moved."

Better than others we know the Judge at whose bar we come to plead. He has chosen us as advocates for our brothers, and He will never leave us without a cause to plead. He knows us well enough to utilize us according to our talents, and even according to our personal preferences.

Religious "advocates" of sinners

For that very reason religious, defendants of so many guilty ones, will have very different ways of understanding their role and their mission as petitioners and suppliants.

There is a very large group to be found among them who feel themselves so thoroughly identified with the Church, our Mother, that they have become incapable of having personal intentions. They leave filially and blindly to the great advocate of Christian people, the great throng of their own children. Is not the Church the true mistress of prayer? Her liturgy makes us pray for the living and the dead. The Pope specifies each year the general and the missionary intentions of the Apostolate of Prayer.

Consecrated souls have no other ambition than to raise their humble voices in a great fraternal choir. They do not doubt that their most intimate requests mount through Christ our Lord to the Almighty Master when their voices are mixed with that of the choir. An antiphon frees them from the least doubt and explains to them how the humblest of supplications can bridge the chasm separating us from the Most High:

> "O Master of all things, Whose throne is in the heavens,
> from which You see all depths, You are the Lord of all
> the chiefs of nations, the poiser of mountains, You Who
> measure the surface of the earth, be understanding and
> favorable to our plaintive sighs." [30]

If one has received by the thousands the confidences of souls of prayer, he is conscious of the right of entertaining this vision: the world is a vast court, and all the religious, dispersed over the whole planet, never cease to plead before God cause of sinners.

In order to win the causes in which they are engaged, they know how to pay the price of them. Before the judges of the tribunals, our advocates lay their talent for speaking, often very powerful. These loving children make with their Father some covenants that are oftentimes heroic. They are ready (with the requisite permissions) to sacrifice all their joys, their liberty, their lives.

Religious "victims" for those dear to them

Their clients come from all environments. Sometimes it is the soul of a father or a mother, or of some well-loved member of the family. The obtaining of the miracle was, in some cases, the motive for their vocation. Considering their prayer insufficient, they have not hesitated to sacrifice all beautiful earthly ambitions. They have offered a life and an apostolate. Many times a day they resume their filial and confident representations in the presence of the Savior of souls. Then they feel they have not given enough, and they contrive to deprive themselves still more, to mortify themselves further by accomplishing all the more perfectly the difficult and complex duties of their state.

This work of winning and redeeming leads these persistent pleaders to explore and discover other heights of greatness. Their familiarity with the Redeemer makes them appreciate experimentally the extent as well as the difficulty of efforts, and the price, the greatness of a human soul, an image of God. By dint of studying the Crucifix and contemplating for a long time its wounds, they have access to a world little known to the masses. Finally it comes to pass that they will be made happy by a total and magnificent victory. This is a marvelous thing: children according to the flesh, religious come to the "spiritual maternity" of their parents.

Harvesters of conversions

These results encourage them, and they apply themselves to appeal in other causes. Now and then time presses, and death threatens a sick person. There are only a few days, sometimes hours, in which to win these desperate causes. The suppliants make themselves even more childlike in calling on their much-loved Father. They have the touching simplicity to review for Him their lives of prayer, and their merits. They have the gift of speaking with the Blessed Virgin, Refuge of Sinners. People claim that some sisters are so holy that they are never unheard in their prayers for conversions. It is their way of arriving at true greatness; that of conquerors who are never defeated.

These "converters" thank the Master of hearts for having put them in the world at this time where, amid incessant struggles and spiritual victories, they can pray for and gain eternal happiness for souls. Success encourages them and widens their ambitions. Victories successfully carried off in their immediate circle of friends, give them the idea and a taste for apostolic campaigns more extensive and farther away.

Apostolic success of contemplatives

The prayer of religious, engaged in all forms of activity, tries to model itself on that of contemplatives. Some well-known facts encourage their hopes. One of the first conquests of a very great "converter," St. Therese de Lisieux, was that of a man condemned to death, who would not have been widely known if his name had not been linked with one of the most popular Saints of the twentieth century.[31] Other conversions, less well known, have been obtained by the religious of the world from God Who gave them in answer to the most loving and generous pleas.

The vast scope of these victories now remains to be specified. We have recalled earlier the mystery hovering over this kind of question. One opinion, often quoted and never found fault with, claims that St. Teresa of Avila in her humble Carmel of St. Joseph as well as in those she founded in Spain in the sixteenth century, had converted as many souls as Saint Francis Xavier, Apostle of the Indies and of Japan, and who died on the shores of China. Has she not written (and we can trust the words of such a saint):

"God withholds Himself from no one who perseveres. He will by little and little strengthen that soul, so that it may come forth victorious. I say resolution, because of the multitude of things which Satan puts before it at first to keep it back from beginning to travel on that road. . . . If he who enters upon this road does violence to himself, with the help of God, so as to reach the summit of perfection, such a one, I believe, will never go to Heaven alone; he will always take many with him. God gives to him, as to a good captain, those who shall be of his company." [32]

When a humble religious can say in confidence and peace that she has been a persuasive advocate before God to obtain from Him the pardon of many sinners, and when she can hope that a goodly number have already crossed the threshold of heaven, she begins to be more conscious that her divine Master has blessed her life. To win, to save souls, to make them aware of the love of God, is the true greatness of an existence. She has accomplished something of eternal value—something real and lasting.

Our God is "trustworthy. By Him you have been called into fellowship with His Son, Jesus Christ, our Lord." [33] All powerful, this God makes certain all the hundredfolds which He has promised. In compensating them for the sacrifice of family and children, He knows how to make of these humble suppliants, queens of the great redeeming people, and He has done so for centuries. It is only in heaven that we shall be able to see the extent as well as the importance of all their spiritual kingdoms.

1 Jeremias, XXIX, 12.

2 Jeremias, II, 13.

3 Isaias, XLV, 22.

4 Isaias, XLV, 6.

5 Osee, VI, 3.

6 Amos, VIII, 11.

7 Psalms, LXI, 9.

8 Sirach, XXIII, 19.

9 I Cor., XIII, 12.

10 Psalms, XXX, 20-21.

11 Psalms, XXIX, 5.

12 Romans, IX, 20-21.

13 Genesis, XXVIII, 12.

14 St. John, XIV, 2.

15 St. Teresa, **Autobiography,** Chapter XXXIV. Cf. text of the Saint, cited by Vacant in **Dict. Théol. Cath.** Mysticism: "The knowledge which the soul acquires in a very short moment, cannot be learned in a thousand years by means of the senses and faculties."

16 Père de Farconet, whom I met at the Chartreuse of Parkminster, England, in 1921.

17 Apoc., IV, 4.

18 Tobias, XII, 12-15.

19 Dom Vallery-Radot: **La Mission de Dom Lehodey.** Ed. Cerf., 1956, p. 63.

20 Robert Oppenheimer.

21 St. Matt., IX, 8.

22 Exodus, XXXII, 12-14.

23 Wisdom, XI, 23-24.

24 Genesis, XVIII, 32.

25 Nehemias, IX, 30.

[26] Jonas, IV, 4.

[27] Ibid., IV, 10.

[28] St. Mark, III, 17.

[29] Vigouroux: **Dictionary of the Bible,** "Boanerges."

[30] Ant. **Magnificat.** Infra hebd. III Nov. Sabbato.

[31] Pranzini, executed at the end of August, 1887.

[32] St. Teresa, **Autobiography,** Chapter XI.

[33] I Cor., I, 9.

CHAPTER VIII

SUFFERING

> "But the God of all grace, who
> has called us unto his eternal glory
> in Christ Jesus, will himself, after
> we have suffered a little while,
> perfect, strengthen and establish
> us." [1]

The religious life is a very beautiful and very noble one because it puts upon us an obligation to make progress in the science of suffering. Like all other disciplines, this one has its beginners, its proficients, its researchers, its pioneers, and its masters. It even has its "doctors." Many of them can be met in the ranks of poor religious, not well educated, but learned in the only science worth while. It is the one which St. Paul tells us surpasses all others:

> "And I brethren, when I came to you, did not come with
> pretentious speech or wisdom announcing unto you the
> witness of Christ. For I determined not to know anything
> among you except Jesus Christ and Him crucified." [2]

In order to deepen the knowledge of the Crucified, religious are ingenious and adaptable.

—They accept and try to love the share of suffering which

their Master has chosen for them whether in the domain of physical suffering or moral distress.

—They enrich themselves during the whole course of their lives by the many sorrowful confidences they receive in their multiple apostolates.

—Solicitous for the beauty and the greatness of souls, they do not hesitate to reveal to them the transforming power of suffering.

I. RELIGIOUS LEARN THROUGH THEIR OWN PERSONAL TRIALS

Revelations concerning physical suffering

The crucifix of a religious is a wonderful book from which she draws a great part of her knowledge of suffering, often varied and profound. When after forty years of consecrated life she looks at it, it brings back to her a whole world of memories. She thinks again of the day of her profession, and especially of the evening when the feast was over and she found herself alone in her little cell with the crucified Friend. The future which awaited her had seemed full of mysteries, but now after half a century of experience, she feels that she has become an expert and an authority on innumerable unhappy people.

She knows that as far as this multitude is concerned, it needs a guide and a model. God has chosen her for this mission and has shown her His beloved Servant:

"And the Lord was pleased to bruise Him in infirmity. . . . If he lay down his life, he shall see a long-lived seed. . . . By his knowledge shall this, my just Servant, justify many, and He shall bear their iniquities upon his shoulders." [3]

Saint Paul completes this by revealing and making exact for her the plan of the Lord:

"For it became Him for whom are all things and through whom are all things, who had brought many sons into glory, to make perfect through sufferings the author of their salvation." [4]

Christ in the world of suffering is still more than in any other, if possible, the sovereignly true Master. To all His disciples whom He invites to ascend toward the transformation effected by suffering, our divine Leader can declare Himself to have surpassed all others—and that by a great deal—in all forms of atrocious physical torture as well as those of measureless spiritual suffering.

Saint Augustine sums up, in his inimitable manner, the meaning and purpose of the Incarnation of the Word:

"Before the Incarnation, God knew physical suffering, but as a spirit, He could not experience it. In order to suffer, one must have a body, and God did not have one. In order to shed blood, one must have blood; to weep, one must have eyes. . . . Beginning from the moment that the Blessed Virgin gave Him a body, Christ became the companion of our suffering. . . . He became a master in all our afflictions. . . . This divine merchant came down from Heaven to our poor earth, a place well endowed, but whose varied riches are destitution, misery, and suffering under all its forms. . . ." [5]

Provided with such keys the religious enters the world of physical suffering. All cases met in the Community infirmaries will appear normal and "necessary." These consecrated persons find it "natural" that all forms as well as all degrees of suffering endured by the poor bodies of their brethren have their counterparts in the flesh of infirm religious. We would think it an anomaly that particularly severe kinds of incurable diseases should not be found among our sick. Some think very simply that the reason they have certain very painful cancers is that God has chosen them for suffering. Certainly there have been and always will be in some of our communities some sufferers whose principal mission will be to share the lot of invalids who are most tried, those for whom sedatives cannot succeed in allaying the pain. Nursing Sisters are the connecting link in the vast and efficacious fraternity of suffering. After having for a long time taken care of cancer patients in her service in the hospital, a sister goes to the infirmary of her community. She gives the same care to one of her companions affected by the same form of cancer, exuding the same pus and giving forth the same odor. When the ravaged features scarcely retain anything human, the nurses seek to find before them the divine beauty of the Leper of Calvary.[6] One of our hospitals has had for some years the impressive statue of Christ the Leper.[7]

Those selected for this most sorrowful companionship, try to murmur between attacks of pain, "It is the Lord; let Him do what is good in His sight."[8] This filial abandonment does not hinder the suffering religious from analyzing very exactly the changes in her long torture. Her eyes fixed on the crucifix, she tries through the mysterious ways of prayer to unite herself to all those with similar sufferings on their beds of torture. They are her people—this race of suffering children. She feels herself at the time their queen and their mother. Speaking their language, powerless to keep back the same moan or even to repress the same cries, she makes known to the Crucified One all the effects of the suffering coming from a paroxysm. When sensibilities are exasperated and insomnia is unconquerable, a moment comes when all control seems to give way. Movements, words, cries, all become incoherent or ungovernable. Minds are ready to break the frontiers of revolt; blasphemies threaten to slip from lips. Understanding the effects of pain, the religious, whose whole body has become a field of torture, begins to plead the cause of the most suffering of her subjects, the most unhappy of her children.

And thus it is that by her merits, she obtains for others that resignation which is impossible or difficult without the aid of a compassionate mother. She knows that certain of her disciples are united with her in her heroism, and thus it is that putting together all forms of torture, she can measure the strength of her supplication—all those appeals and all those cries which she makes go up to the Crucified Master. She discovers at the same time the reason for her sublime vocation. God has chosen her, He has preferred her to so many others to be the animating spirit, the soul of all that vast army of martyrs. It is under this form and through this way that her religious life itself leads to beauty and mounts toward grandeur.

Moral suffering

The crown of thorns of the Crucifix symbolizes humiliations, defeats, reputations sacrificed, and honor definitely lost. Humble and loyal disciples of their Master, King of the humiliated, religious fear to be incompetent and without authority among the defeated victims whom they meet in their apostolates. They insistently beg of their Friend to let them know through experience all that the human heart can suffer from muliplied failures and the slow but certain loss of all kinds of respect. And the Lord, Who seeks for those who will reproduce or continue His sufferings, who are capable of reliving most humiliating conditions, calls upon generous souls.

When these sought-for experiences commence for them, fervent religious soon become aware that the liveliest and best-endowed imagination remains powerless to give any idea of the frightful solitude wherein live the humiliated and dishonored. Worlds like these, though populated by thousands, are practically unknown to those who have never dwelt there. Nothing can inform "strangers" about the calamities which must be lived. No one has ever made profound studies of the psychology of the unfortunate. Only they themselves could tell their own stories, but they have neither the courage nor the strength to do so.

However, because the sons of God are dressed like Christ in the white robe of the fool,[8b] they have a right to be visited by expert consolers who speak their language, after having gone through their ordeal. The almost intolerable sufferings endured by religious who are victims of defeat, calumny, and even dishonor, can find there a providential explanation. It is good to know that consecrated souls can reach that height of heroism. Having verified by experience that the victims of dishonor refuse all comfort from those who have not experienced their sorrow or from those who do not know the taste of complete bitterness, religious are loving enough to beg Christ of the Agony to let them drink the dregs of His chalice. They are well enough loved to have their desires granted.

II. THE SCIENCE OF SUFFERING GATHERED THROUGH MULTIPLE CONFIDENCES

From the apostles of common people

Poor neighborhoods have their dramas which the *Visitors* of the poor and the sick know well. For the glory of the Church, our good and tender Mother, the unwritten history of suffering of the poor has many a time found place and refuge in the compassionate hearts of very holy religious.[9]

In a world where justice, and above all kindness, are still far from being supreme, there dwell legions of the poor and humble who have not awakened interest or pity in any of their fellowmen. It is, however, in the ranks of these seemingly insignificant beings, that those could be recruited who would glorify the Eternal:

"Who shall glorify Thee more, O Sovereign Master? The soul that is sorrowful for the evil she has done, and goes forth bowed down and feeble. . . . The hungry soul giveth glory and justice to Thee, O Lord." [10]

Every nation furnishes its contingent of unfortunates, doomed to effacement and to insignificance even if contempt has spared them. Common traits draw them together in the fraternity of misery. Often not very intellignt, somewhat unskilled, they have to be indefinitely occupied with routine tasks and wearisome work in order to eke out an existence. They are resigned to work which will keep them from dying of hunger, but how can they be resigned to callous, universal indifference? For years they have met thousands of passersby, and in no face have they detected a spark of interest, or a smile of kindness. Ah! There is at least one science which they possess in its perfection. On the human faces turned toward them, they can see shades of expression which they recognize as severity, harshness, disdain, or contempt. Beyond these cruel glances, they see manifested in the onlookers' faces the wicked joy that they do not belong to such a vulgar crowd. The human soul has an extraordinary power to bear for a lifetime the weight of such keen suffering! If at least the unfortunate knew how to be sufficiently fraternal, they could carry together the weighty common cross.[10b]

Too often, terrible loneliness is added to this incredible trial. May God give us hearts kind enough to become exceedingly wise in the little known world of man's suffering! We should discover in alarm all the resentment that wells up in embittered hearts during long evenings and interminable nights:

"What shall glorify Thee . . . the broken heart . . . and the hungry soul."

The Lord, sublime Friend of the unfortunate, does not remain deaf to these piercing cries. Again let us not hesitate to praise the splendor of our consecrated lives. The explanation of some vocations found therein is simple and divine. An unfortunate person has never succeeded in overcoming the indifference of others, but a religious offers herself to God in order to become a loving mother to the humiliated. Her apostolate will honor her and transport her to the land of miracles. Endowed with extraordinary patience, a true gift of God, she will listen during the course of many years to the interminable life stories of many "little" ones. She is the only one in the world who interests herself enough to listen to the end to these humble but overwhelming tragedies. She knows them and relives them just as they lived them before telling them to her. When she is there, bearing with a flood of bitter complaints, when she hears rebellion threatening, she feels herself a messenger of the pity of God. She thanks Him for having chosen her from among so many others, to be placed where she can show the tenderness of God to be visible and near.

Her recompense, she feels, is touching and magnificent. One never will know the world of beauty in souls until he has seen the very first smile dawn on a human face, the one brought by the living and faithful image of the goodness of God. This spectacle is a familiar one to religious, visitors of the poor, in overcrowded quarters of the poor everywhere. How many times that sight is renewed for them, but always more and more enriched with untold details. Mothers know well that each child has for them a smile particularly its own, and which she knows is incessantly enriched and embellished. In making known to the unfortunate the kindness from which they have been cut off, the religious remains, with God, the sole witness of something sublime. A person lives, under her eyes, through the most extraordinary minute of its whole existence. For the sinner it is a passage from darkness into light, and sometimes the instant of his entrance into the Kingdom of God, or his return to the house of his Father. For thirty or forty years, he has never seen any but indifferent or scornful faces, some harsh and full of hatred, and suddenly he sees on a pure human face the first reflection of the beauty of God. It is for hundreds of hours such as this that God has chosen us. It is another of our hundredfolds.

We offer Him our lives, and in a magnificent recompense, truly worthy of His unbound goodness, the Lord lets us find that secret door opening into privileged regions where dwell the most beautiful souls in the world. It is a privilege to be put in a position to study at length even one superb soul. One of the advantages of the religious life is to be able to meet nobility and moral victories by the hundreds.

Knowledge of suffering learned by educators

By dint of contemplating the wound in the side of Christ, opening on His pierced Heart, religious, unwearied explorers of the suffering of their brethren, arrive at other shores, those of the country overpopulated with poorly loved or unloved persons.

But, as we have said before, educators have the beautiful mission of teaching their pupils to love. In sad counterpart, it very often happens that they have to be concerned with complex situations in which the victims are the poorly-loved. There are always many unhappy young girls. They do not receive from their parents the elementary love to which they have a right, and they show themselves to be cynical and bitter. Tactful religious, friends of God and of youth, know how to dress these wounds. They do so in such a way that these neglected girls will learn how to save their own children later on from the great evil of which they were the victims.

Very often teachers are sought out by their former pupils who have been used roughly by life. How often young wives have not found with their chosen companion in life the reward of the beautiful love which they brought to him! They weep at the frightful prospect of a long life without love. The enriched experience of religious, confidants of souls by the hundreds, makes it possible for them to recall many other cases, sadly analogous. Examples also, verging on the sublime, are drawn from the treasury of their memories, and they can show a way in which these lives, through heroism, can become fruitful.

Mothers who are unloved

Unhappier very often is the case of poor mothers who, however devoted they may be, cannot succeed in winning their children's affection. The love that religious bear to Christ and to unhappy persons gives them a psychology rich enough and flexible enough to adapt themselves to innumerable cases, but each one unique, that come to them for consolation.

A religious teacher, disciple of the Virgin of Pity, knows how to compassionate these unloved mothers. They feel, women and mothers themselves, how horrible it would be for a mother not to be loved. The deepest and purest desire would find itself abominably frustrated. A teacher perceives to what extent such a blow would be tragic and monstrous. Her virginity has left her or made her human and tender. She knows how to offer adequate sympathy, and the voluntary sacrifice which she had the strength to make of the joys of a family, confers on her the authority and right to assure the sufferer that even without the just and sweet recompense of love a devotedness remains possible—total, disinterested, and heroic, if necessary.

III. SUFFERING MAGNIFIES THE HUMAN SOUL

To all the advantages already pointed out, the religious life adds one privilege more, and it is an enviable one. It permits us to see at close range the most brilliant and the most glorious triumphs of souls. The most difficult and the most beautiful of these victories are won in the domain of forgiveness. The great God wishes to associate His beloved children in His own greatness. In order to do this, He proposes to them His own Son as a model for their imitation. The greatest victory gained by the soul of Christ was the complete pardon which He accorded to His executioners:

"Father, forgive them, for they know not what they do." [11]

This utterance has been immensely fruitful. All Christians who bring themselves to heroic forgiveness, even to love of their former enemies, could have done these things only through imitating their Model. St. Thomas Aquinas has said that

". . . the love of enemies is an action so difficult that God alone could have the right to ask such a thing." [12]

Pardon for torturers

The race of unfeeling brutes is not wiped off the earth. In this new generation, these strange people still count thousands of individuals. They are said to be ingenious in their horrible discoveries. They seem to overlook nothing in the dark history of the barbarity of man. But, as in other sciences, this one seems to have made gigantic advances in the last few decades. Heads of state and technicians have become great masters in the technique of punishment. They are doctors of cruelty; they seem proud of their title and of their unheard-of achievements.

God alone knows the number of their victims. Religious have prayed to obtain choice places in the new generation of martyrs. It appears strange to them to be spared when others of their race enrich at their expense the science of modern torture, surpassing even their sorrowful predecessors. There are religious in the Church of Silence who have already spent many years in captivity. They know all too well the labyrinth of their caves, mysterious to the majority of our contemporaries. They live near enough to the torture chambers to hear the terrible cries of those punished. Victims themselves, they have become learned in a rather rare science, and their experiences have made them extraordinarily compassionate.

When the tortured come to them, groaning, weeping, and bleeding, they can see on their lips, murmured in a sigh, perfect pardon and deep love for the pitiless brutes. Tears, blood, and gaping wounds tell better the heroism of their prayers. God is, as it were, within them to bring His light, His pardon, and His peace to executioners.

Some may be set free, and the inhuman governments disappear, but they still keep in their flesh, like the martyrs of the first ages, the stigmata of the tortures endured for Christ. But what they cannot forget are the deaths they have witnessed of so many victims. Their quarters were often in common and they could hear the moans, the sighs, and sometimes also cries of revolt, and threats of fury and vengeance. And yet in complete contrast there were other victims who, having endured the same punishments, rose from the abyss of their misery to the heights of love. In spite of the prospect of shortened lives or of incurable disease, they accepted and offered all to God as a ransom for these heartless souls. They never thought they had paid too high a price for light, peace, and joy. For even of these cruel executioners they dreamed of making children of God, and even martyrs for Christ. How grand is the vocation that makes us witnesses and sometimes artisans of sublimity!

Pardon for despoilers and destroyers of virtue

In the beautiful world of magnanimous souls, there are other pardons with other glories. Religious have often been the sole witnesses of them—and with priests—the sole confidants.

Resourceful servants of all forms of the mercy of God, they call together in their welcoming houses the victims and the wrecks of vice. The sensibilities of the latter, so long in revolt, have made them hate and curse their former associates for profaning their virtue, destroying their ideals, and ravaging their peace. Then, in daily contact with a religious, always kind and never contemptuous, they begin again to rediscover a soul under the ruins of an apparently wasted life. Those who are shut in like prisoners, after having been violated, put themselves under the tutelage of the "Sisters"— that is the name they give them.

Little by little they begin to find out that the "Mothers" —still another one of their names—have given up the finest of human lives and the most promising of earthly prospects in order to become, by vocation and preference, their voluntary companions, their friends. Some of these religious have an exceptional knowledge of wretchedness. Their hearts are

full of the histories of poor lives. A long and extensive experience provided a solid basis for their valuable learning in pity.
They are above all admirably prudent, following the Scrip-
tural injunction:

"Let anything you hear die within you." [13]

As a result of the fullness of these discoveries and of all
the silent testimonies of kindness, a barrier begins to rise
against hatred. An entirely new light comes into the soul
and unsuspected possibilities open before it. The victim
begins to see, little by little, that the weak, those whose passions have overcome reason, have made slaves of themselves.
She tells herself that the unfortunate are only pitiable creatures. In the hierachy of courage and moral grandeur, it is
this lamentable group that has the lowest place. Her heart,
become kind, does not curse the poor and no longer scorns
the weak. She has ceased to rejoice with a wicked joy on
seeing this enemy overcome, crushed, and humiliated. When
she understands all this distress, and knows it to be, as it
were, ingrained in a person and in his life, then she enter-
tains for him an unwavering pity, and exerts all her ingenuity
to bring him help. A door commences to open on an unknown
world. A truth makes itself clear, a discovery comes to "lib-
erate" her: the true greatness is that of souls.

The "Magdalens" of yesterday dream of preparing for
this grandeur hundreds of weak people whom they met in
the days of their folly. Believing now in the Almighty power
of God, in the immense love which He bears to souls created
in His image, they beg Him to change the hearts whose weakness they have measured. They pray, they suffer, in order
that an ideal may rise like a dawn of hope in these poor, skep-

tical, and bitter hearts. They ask God to be merciful enough to drive out that misery which has impoverished them so much.

The triumph of beauty in the world of souls is what we must contemplate. It is a privilege all too rare to witness the transformation of an existence by God, and to follow all its advances from the abyss of moral misery to heroism and real sanctity. Religious follow or guide these souls in their spiritual journeys. The surroundings can be commonplace and austere. On these beds of the sick ward repose, grouped together in their common dishonor, the poor victims of the frailty of mankind. Wounds of the body are incurable, and the scars of vice uneffaceable. But in these poor bodies wonderful souls have been reborn and now flourish, those which in the hierarchy of spiritual beauty move more rapidly towards the highest perfection.

Long ago these victims had pardoned the brutal men, but why should they limit themselves to that action now found to be elementary. They make notable advances into the regions of moral splendor. They dream of multiplying those who walk on the roads which lead to the marvelous country. They entreat God, and not only by prayer but by the heroic offering of all the wounds of their profaned and bruised flesh, to dry up in hearts the source of weakness and to send down floods of grace and light. Souls become very holy in making themselves the "redemptresses" of despoilers and killers of virtue.

Prudent religious rally them and help to direct their prayer. They thank their Master for having put them at the meeting place of so many wonders. Demonstrations become superfluous for these privileged witnesses of all these splendid moral victories. They know for a fact from unmistakable evidence that physical and moral suffering works marvels and magnifies lives, from the time a sincere being lets itself be carried away by the Divine Artisan Who uses hearts in His crucible. When drawn together by the common love of God, souls become united and rival one another in striving to reach the Divine Beauty of which they are very faithful copies among us. These religious and their disciples now go forward in a fraternal group toward vital discoveries. This is the admirable world now become familiar to religious everywhere. They thank God for having taken them from an ordinary and uneventful life in order to make them artisans and witnesses of the most amazing spiritual victories possible of achievement. They feel very intensely that the common environment in which they will have passed their lives is one of the spiritual high spots in the world of souls. When, in their prayers, they recall all that they have seen and observed: miraculous conversions, radical transformations, spiritual regenerations, heroic and saintly deaths—they are overwhelmed by gratitude. It is because the Redeemer has loved them so much that He has associated them efficaciously with His enterprises of pardon and ransom.

Superb words have always been spoken, but no trace of some of them is preserved in any human book. Humble religious keep in their hearts unforgettable formulas. They cannot praise God enough for the marvels which He has worked everywhere and at all times in the hearts of His friends. It is impossible for these privileged witnesses to entertain thoughts of pessimism. The work of the Lord is a magnificent success. The splendor of His beauty shines over all human souls everywhere. The multitudes, of which the first group were those once gathered at the Mount of the Beatitudes, have come down through the generations. No force, no violence, no regime has yet been able to extinguish the fire which Jesus came to cast upon the earth.[14] The flame may diminish so low as to be no more than a flicker, but we have the certitude that nothing or no one can extinguish it.

There are numbers of privileged religious who pass their lives near this frontier which is continually crossed by those who "go up from shadows toward His marvelous light." [15]

How could one ever regret having sacrificed all when she finds her place in this beautiful universe of souls, of these souls who are images and daughters of God!

---

[1] I Peter, V, 10.

[2] I Cor., II, 1-2.

[3] Isaias, LIII, 10-11.

[4] Hebrews, II, 10.

[5] Texts from readings in St. Augustine.

[6] Isaias, LIII, 4; St. Matt., VIII, 17.

[7] Briode. The image has been taken from the hospital to the Basilica of Saint-Julien.

[8] I Samuel, III, 18.

[8b] St. Luke, XXIII, 11.

[9] We have no right to overlook the admirable devotedness of so many social workers. Many of them are themselves among the "consecrated." Cf. J. M. Perrin: **Consecration a Dieu et Presence au Monde,** Desclée de Brouwer.

[10] Baruch, II, 18.

[10b] Galatians, VI, 2.

[11] St. Luke, XXIII, 34.

[12] IIa-IIae, quest. 27, art. 7.

[13] Sirach, XIX, 9.

[14] St. Luke, XII, 49.

[15] I Peter, II, 9.

CHAPTER IX

THE APOSTOLATE

"O Divine Fire, stir up in all those
who have part in Thy apostolate,
the flames that transformed those
fortunate retreatants in the Upper
Room." [1]

Since they are children of God, daughters of the Church,
and friends of souls, religious are normally apostles. A goodly
number of them suffer from a happy obsession regarding the
salvation of their brethren, and it is there that we must look
for the origin of their manifold apostolates.

The personal apostolate of religious, sometimes carried
on in many countries, brings them a spiritual family, constantly being increased. They will know only in Heaven
the extent and the importance of their conquests. Some of
the apostles have their favorite children, for example, the
weak or the victims of dishonor.

God, contemplated and prayed to, makes them more and
more familiar with His spirit. He reveals to them the great
laws of the Father's methods of teaching. He enriches them
with a growing participation in His attributes. He teaches
them to be patient, merciful, and tender to the children of
men. He gives them the courage and strength to carry on
harassing and often gigantic enterprises.

The Church of Christ stirs up its children to that catholicity so much recommended by its Master. Religious become familiar with the divine idea of the universal brotherhood of all human races. Their prayer and their apostolate as well are stimulated by cosmic purposes and visions.

I. PERSONAL APOSTOLATES

"As one face differs from another, so does one human heart from another." [2]

The apostles must then apply themselves to adaptations which are constantly changing. This calls for a universal ascese for workers anxious to succeed with all the opportunities offered. Reality, always surprising, often demands servitude and slavery. It will sometimes be a question of sacrificing a much cherished personality which, being too forceful, is likely to interpose a separation between God and souls.

A religious should be careful above all to free herself from domineering attitudes. She must patiently keep herself as a listener, on the same level as the ignorant and the retarded. There is a sacred and beautiful tradition among all teaching religious: no child must be neglected. Those least endowed become the object of a maternal solicitude. Religious never weary of repeating the same thing, and they are clever in finding out or in devising sometimes very simple ways of making these pupils understand. This laborious but very efficacious pedagogy becomes that of the apostles.

Inaptitudes or intellectual deficiencies are not the only obstacles holding back the advance of the truth to souls. The poor and humble are often timid, sensitive, and wary, and they need apostles who are experienced in mildness.

A Christian of the 17th century did not hesitate to say to one of his pupils at the opening of his apostolic career, which became a particularly efficacious one:

"In order to do good to the neighbor, one needs mildness no less than patience." [3]

This paternal advice was formulated a few years after the death of St. Francis de Sales, whose gentleness was achieved and maintained through many heroic struggles.

Personal conquests

The solidarity between Christians is universal and complex. Conversions therefore are the result of incalculable influences and causes. The treasury of the Communion of Saints belongs to everyone in a fraternal collectivity. But in the ascent of the blind toward the light, in the journeys and the wanderings of the prodigals toward their Father's home, there are dominant and determining influences. Sinners or unbelievers remember all their lives the name of the apostle who led them into the fold. Others, overwhelmed by a remorse as severe as unforeseen, inspired by an imperious longing for innocence and divine things, will never know on earth the country or the nationality of their mysterious converters.

Those who in unconscious and touching simplicity have become gradually kings or queens of a great nation of ransomed souls are living unknown in their cells, or in their humble employments. "To serve God is to become a leader of a nation." How can any apostle, become the joyous shepherd of a vast flock, ever call by name the sheep and the lambs? But the Good Shepherd can call "his own sheep by name." [4]

First of all, there may be some faraway ancestors who have benefitted by the retroactive effects of the prayer and suffering of one of their descendants. Then there are all those persons who were as children stamped for life with the impress of a teacher who lived the virtues she taught. No one can tell the number of sick attended, nor of the humble, the little ones, the poor of upright heart, all those who seek God, who have been called together from so many "tribes and countries" by obscure shepherds, purveyors of light.

When at night in great motherhouses, or in communities on the missions, or in villages so many unknown religious fall asleep, marvels continue to be carried on in the crowds starved for truth. Desires are aroused and revived, advances made to moral beauty, and progress goes forward toward the sanctity of God.

On the quest for "lost sheep"

Faithful to the spirit and the preference of her Master, the religious apostle interests herself in that portion of the multitude especially cherished since the message of the Beatitudes: all those who possess some degree of poverty. How many missionaries have repeated in their hearts the expression of their desires: "Henceforth, I shall go to the Gentiles." [5]

How many apostles have never had to leave their country, having found within easy reach victims of all kinds of spiritual poverty. Let us call to mind the great number of the weak and the solitary poor whom shame has driven away and excluded from the companionship of their neighbors and friends.

The weak

The Creator of all forms of mercy endows the heart of His apostles with all the gradations of His kindness. On each new day, mindful of the unfortunate who await them, God is pleased to reveal to religious some aspects, still unknown, of the kindness of the Father. And those sent by the good Master will, with open hands, scatter new riches on the weak, assuring them of unlimited power to reclaim themselves. Each day of apostolic labor confirms these envoys in a double assurance. Human weakness is found to be the same in every continent. For twenty centuries, to be exact, all the people of the world, as in the time of the Gospel, find among themselves replicas of the Magdalen, the Prodigal Son, the hard-hearted rich, the unfaithful servants, and the foolish virgins.

In the world of the weak, as in others, each one lives in his destitution in his own personal way. In the school of these experiences which are constantly renewed and revivified the knowledge of apostles can become prodigious. A sister, a real friend of the souls of her brethren, could no longer be astonished at the unbelievable cleverness of sinners in doing evil. Having gathered so many testimonies and witnessed so much weakness, she has learned that a human being can be settled in his sin, and take pleasure there. He can extinguish in his own heart even the desire to be exorcized of it.

The occupations and the apostolic enterprises of religious leave them scarcely any time available for reading the history of kings. However, they would scarcely be shocked by the revelations that would come to them of moral distress of long standing in the most illustrious courts. Louis XIV acknowledged to his mother that

> "he had done what he could to keep himself from offending God in not abandoning himself to his passions; but he was forced to acknowledge to her that they had become stronger than his reason, that he could not resist their violence, and that he did not even feel the desire to do so." [6]

It is not necessary to explain at length to "doctors" in the science of the weak that the most solemn exhortations made to sinners are scarcely ever efficacious. In 1666 the dying Queen said again to her son:

> "Do what I have told you. I say it to you again with the Blessed Sacrament on my lips." [7]

History tells us that twenty years went by before the supplications of a mother in her agony became finally efficacious.

Religious specializing in the apostolate for the weak have a particular devotion to the infinite patience of God. Poor sinners feel them to be gracious and understanding, and often tell them things which they would not even tell their mothers. It sometimes happens that these apostles reap the first fruits of some avowals even before the priests do. An old author tells us of that Father of the Church who "made of his heart a true library of Jesus Christ."

After some years of apostolic work, the hearts of certain religious are veritable living jewel cases. As others carry jewels, they carry treasures of hundreds of stories, very often some dreadful ones. No one will ever write them, but they were lived by a poor human being and the confidante who received them does not tangle up this horribly complicated skein any more than God does. This is the food on which the religious nourishes her prayer. It is about these poor and sad things that religious speak to Christ and to His Mother when prudently and silently they "go out quickly into the streets and lanes of the city and bring in the poor, and the crippled, and the blind, and the lame." [8]

The victims of dishonor

There are some houses which, though not haunted, are never visited any more. No one ever crosses their thresholds. This is because shame has come upon the inhabitants of these sad dwellings. They have withdrawn themselves into a fearful solitude. Should one go to express his sympathy or simply his pity, he would risk defilement; and to write them or to telephone them appears to be imprudent. Behind shutters which are often closed, a symbol of definite grief, these unfortunates live throughout the day, weighed down with the tedium of life, and by night are victims of unconquerable insomnia. They feel that never again will they recover the good opinion of men. Everything is lost, honor above all, and they dream of suicide.

One day a religious visitor comes in, prudent, compassionate, full of interest and rich in pity. The well-known habit which she wears, the outward sign of her dedication, gives her the right to cross all thresholds. Without defiling herself, she can approach the impure. Dishonor and shame can never bespatter her. It is the Originator and Creator of pity Who sends her, Who employs her in the search for all the lost souls,[9] and "for all who are being lost." [10]

She is a very compassionate ambassadress of the King Who does not always ratify the sentence of men, nor treat with severity the repentant heart which turns again to love.

II. LESSONS OF DIVINE PEDAGOGY

"But when thou prayest, go into thy room and closing thy door, pray to thy Father in secret; and thy Father Who sees in secret will reward thee." [11]

The complete gift of one's self to others and all the great manifestations of zeal are born of these intimacies. One could not occupy herself with souls for any length of time without learning the lessons of the Heavenly Father. No one is good if he has not drunk deeply at the only source of all goodness, for "One only is good." [12]

From the source of all these gifts the apostles ought to draw the courage, the endurance, and the independence which they need to carry on their apostolic endeavors:

"Pray at all times in the spirit, and be therein vigilant in all perseverance and supplication for all the Saints, and for me when I open my mouth that utterance may be granted me fearlessly to make known the mystery of the gospel, for which I am an ambassador in chains, so that therein I may dare to speak as I ought." [13]

"For I have not shrunk from declaring to you the whole counsel of God." [14]

"But with me it is a very small matter to be judged by
you or any man's tribunal. . . . He Who judges me is the
Lord." [15]

In the long hours of prayerful intimacy, hearts grown
familiar with the Eternal God, discover one after another,
the laws of His paternal pedagogy. God is the Creator, the
Friend of each of the souls of men. The salvation of the
people of earth is the permanent concern of the Father of
all. Spring brings us each year the touching image of this
divine two-fold care. The sap does not neglect the smallest
branch, the most hidden bud receives its share. Whole continents re-awaken, flourish, and renew their life.

The prayer of apostles is regulated and modeled by
the love which God lets fall at times on certain individuals
and on all humanity. After having pleaded and won the
cause of a sinner in agony, a religious unknown to the world,
lets herself be raised by her Father to magnificent visions
with which He does not hesitate to associate her. In his contemplation of the Incarnation, St. Ignatius invites us

"to see, to look for some time at the Three Divine Persons. Under their gaze, the face of the earth lies open,
and the immensity of its continents is spread out. . . .
God lets fall His mercy on the whole human race." [16]

The apostles of our generation feel that if they were
united to such a good Father, it would be possible for them
to enter into mysterious contact with the three thousand
millions of beings making up the human race today. The
Friend Who is so near, so tenderly paternal, is He Who has

created all these souls in a majestic rhythm of about five hundred thousand a day.

> "God must love the common people, since He made so many of them." [17]

The Creator nourishes these bodies, He makes them live. His Son has "shed His blood for their redemption." [18]
"God, our Savior, wishes all men to be saved and to come to the knowledge of the truth." [19]
Saint Paul enjoins us that absolutely no one should be excluded from our prayers:

> "I urged you, therefore, first of all, that supplications and intercessions . . . be made for all men, for Kings and all in high positions." [20]

This plan of apostolic prayer governs all requests of religious. Masters more or less popular among people today have their daily and generous part in the ardent supplications of the humble. Dictators are neither forgotten nor excluded. How many of our martyrs have offered their sufferings and their lives that God would pour His light and love into the hard hearts of their persecutors.

The history of the destiny of souls that could never be written would reveal hundreds of amazing secrets. Some atrociously cruel leaders, hated by the people whom they oppress, will perhaps owe their salvation to obscure suppliants, incapable of hatred. The knowledge of the mercy and pity of God, in the course of ages, has borne fruit. Fortunate are the apostolates whose source is in God!

III. UNIVERSALITY OF THE APOSTOLATES

The great multitude of a million religious plays, at all times, a decisive role in the universal family of souls. Many of those who pray have never left their monastery, where for thirty and forty years, they have kept their vow of stability. Their compatriots, sometimes village folk, yet Catholics, live in narrow streets. They bring suit to settle petty joint ownerships, they cling passionately to the bit of earth which has become their own after grinding labor. They declare themselves satisfied and feel so. Thus they pass their lives, as limited in their hopes as they are in their desires. Their intentions in prayer scarcely go outside the circle of relatives and friends, living or dead.

However, their daughters and sisters may have a country, a continent, and an entire world [19b] continually in their prayers. This is one of the successes of the maternal pedagogy of the Church. To the greater part of her religious she has given a soul, universal and genuinely Catholic.

Religious, familiar with the Gospel and so many of the sacred texts, understand that their apostolate can and should extend to the whole inhabited earth.

"Are you not the children of the prophets and of the covenant that God made with your fathers, saying to Abraham: And in thy offspring shall all the families of the earth be blessed." [21]

We know that thanks to Jesus, Savior of mankind, God offers now the promises He made to the Chosen People to a world-wide Israel. The magnificent and enviable prayers made by the Jews in the time of the Machabees can be repeated in our days in favor of all men.

> "O Lord God, Creator of all things, dreadful and strong, just and merciful, Who alone art the good King, Who alone art gracious, Who alone art just, and almighty and eternal, Who deliverest Israel from all evil, Who didst choose the fathers, and didst sanctify them; receive the sacrifices for all thy people Israel, and preserve Thy own portion and sanctify it." [22]

The apostles are convinced that the Gospel message is destined for all.

> "Go into the whole world and preach the Gospel to every creature." [23]

Because

> ". . . Jesus was to die not only for the nation, but that He might gather into one the children of God who were scattered abroad." [24]

Therefore,

> "To you is the promise and to your children, and to those who are far off, even to all whom the Lord our God calls to Himself." [25]

Does not St. Peter say:

> "Now I really understand that God is not a respecter of

persons, but in every nation, he who fears Him and does what is right is acceptable to Him." [26]

Even "to the gentiles also God has given repentance unto life." [27]

Because they are solidly aligned to the views and the will of their Father, religious have mapped out their apostolates. They thank God for having delivered them from narrow views, deep set prejudices, and atavistic racialism. They surrender without reserve to the transforming love that dwells in them. They receive their large share of His universal benevolence. In their pursuits and explorations as apostles, they let themselves be guided by the Savior of souls.

A religious, sent by her Master, feels ready and disposed for all kinds of missions. The earthly country of the human being given her in her apostolate matters little to her. Nothing can offend her in this child of God, no matter what was the culture of his ancestors, their poverty, or the insignificance of his own tribe. It is with the same faith and the same love that she goes into the tropical jungles or the igloo of the polar snows.[27b] This universal friend of souls has no trouble in persuading herself that the unknown whom she addresses, the one whose name no archivist will ever keep or inscribe, is truly a cherished child of the Creator. She discovers in a blessed enlightenment that God has detached her from any continent in order that her path might one day cross that of this new child, coming toward her in an inexplicable mystery.

Love knows no frontiers or limits

Apostles, privileged servants of the Lord, come to this astonishing conviction: their love for their fellowmen ought to be without barriers or limits. It is not necessary to remind them with insistence of the proclamation of St. Paul to the Galatians:

"For you are all children of God through faith in Christ Jesus. For all you who have been baptized into Christ have put on Christ. There is neither Jew nor Greek, nor slave nor freeman . . . for you are all one in Christ Jesus." [28]

We know that we cannot misrepresent the thought or the commissions of the great Apostle, although they are twenty centuries old, in translating them into the language of our generation, in bringing out their ardent timeliness. May it no longer be a question among Christians of our day whether persons are American, Russian, or Chinese, any more than French or German, Spaniards or Brazilian, Arabs or Jews. May opposition between workers and owners cease. May there be a truce to making distinctions between privileged and inferior nations. White men are the human brothers of the colored people of all races. No more may the poor be lined up against the rich, and the great of this world despise and humiliate the common people. When will the brahmins become truly the brothers of the pariahs? Will the world continue to despise the blacks or the pygmies? One same baptism makes us the children of the same Father. We have become, as Pius XII said, "universal brothers." Let us try, with grace, to develop within ourselves and to obtain a "universal soul."

These slogans which entire people hesitate to make their own, and to which they can scarcely rally a large number of Catholics, are the ones our religious live up to everywhere.

We find our religious in the great ports of the world where the races of the world rub elbows, and in the much more cosmopolitan capitals. Here teachers as well as hospital nurses devote their lives to children, to the sick, the wounded, and to the aged of all nations represented at the United Nations or the UNESCO. The color of the faces matters not at all to them; they see only the well-loved children of the Father of all mankind. Reflexive instincts, atavistic revulsions no longer exist; they are all mastered and vanquished. The triumphant love of their God has put into the hearts of religious the spirit of fraternity and tenderness which might be proclaimed "miraculous" since they remain so very much the lot of the elite.

Visions and cosmic prayers

Ever more closely united to God, our lives ascend still higher on the way to beauty and grandeur. Some religious, without remarkable education, entertain cosmic visions. The figures and the speculations of the demographers lift them up to sublime prayer.

In communities counting few members, persons who are trifling with their eternal destiny are constantly prayed for. The fullness and the surplus of our supplications build up a prayer which will be welcome to the nations that the curves of statistics aid us to foresee.

The most numerous people on earth, the six hundred millions of Chinese, might count, towards the end of the century, a billion people. The fervent prayers sent up to God in favor of this mass of humanity "will permit" the Friend of souls to utilize these appeals for the elect of His choice, to distribute among them the graces of light, heroism, and sanctity. For these apostles, ambitious for great fulfillments and spiritual marvels, carry powerful hopes in their hearts. Religious are strongly persuaded that all races and nations of the world will see saints and patrons coming from their ranks and their lineage. They will have had their share, humble but certain, in the success and triumphs of the most exalted members of the human race.

When a periodical or a review publishes figures, stating that there will be world populations of five to six billion people by the end of the twentieth century, those who pray, without any publicity, filially speak to God about the unimaginable needs of the Church, their Mother, after the year 2000.

As the hours and the days go by, "saints" of the nations are called by God "out of darkness into His marvelous light." [29]

They penetrate into the splendors of truth, they cross the threshold of charity. Rancors are done away with; hatreds are vanquished. The sad and monotonous experiences of lust are replaced in hearts with the uplifting longing for purity. The aged, at the end of life, see truth shine forth; the weak and the humiliated receive installments from the infinite kindness of God through the hands and care of His faithful servants.

The migrants towards the light come from all environments and all countries. No one notes down these marvels; nothing can measure the amplitude and the power of these spiritual tides. The world will not remain the same after the passage among us of sincere and genuine apostles.

[1] The Soul of the Apostolate, Chautard.

[2] Proverbs, XXVII, 19.

[3] Xav. Séjourne, S.J., Histoire du Bienheureux Jul. Maunoir, Poitiers, 1895, p. 35.

[4] St. John, X, 3.

[5] Acts, XVIII, 6.

[6] Mme. de Motteville, confidante of Anne of Austria, Memoirs.

[7] Ibid.

[8] St. Luke, XIV, 21-23.

[9] Ezech., XXXIV, 16.

[10] St. Matt., XVIII, 11.

[11] St. Matt., VI, 6.

[12] St. Matt., XIX, 17.

[13] Ephesians, VI, 19-20.

[14] Acts, XX, 27.

[15] I Cor., IV, 3-4.

[16] Spiritual Exercises. Cf. Psalms XXXII, 13-15: "From heaven to earth the Lord looks down; He sees all mankind, He Who fashioned the heart of each, He Who knows all their works."

[17] Abraham Lincoln, president of the United States (1860-65).

[18] St. Matt., XXVI, 28.

[19] I Tim., II, 3-4.

[20] Ibid., II, 1-2.

[20b] The Buddhists of Hiroshima expressed this request: "You have religious who kneel daily to ask God's help. We should like to have Catholic religious who would pray without ceasing for the peace of the world." C. C. C., April, 1959.

[21] Acts, III, 25.

[22] II Machabees, I, 24-26.

[23] St. Mark, XVI, 15.

[24] St. John, XI, 52.

[25] Acts, II, 39.

[26] Acts, X, 35.

[27] Acts, XI, 18.

27b Missi, Oct. 1959: "Our Lady of the Snows," a congregation recently founded for young Eskimo girls at Nome, Alaska. In 1959, an Ursuline religious had spent 36 years in apostolic work in the Great North.

28 Gal., III, 26-28.

29 I Peter, II, 9.

CHAPTER X

THE GOOD TREE BRINGETH FORTH GOOD FRUIT [1]

> "It is now forty years that God has been with you." [2]
>
> "The desire for wisdom leads to a kingdom. If then you find pleasure in throne and scepter, honor wisdom that you may reign forever." [3]

The infinite beauty of God shines over all creation. Landscapes bathed in light are the diminished reflections of His splendor. In the world of souls, divine beauty becomes living and striking. At the end of life, after spiritual and moral success, human souls exhibit all the heavenly beauty with which they have been clothed. They make incarnate the kindness, patience, and mercy of the Father Whom they have loved.

The religious life, together with the sacerdotal life, gives us convincing proofs of these peace-producing certainties:

1. In the still unfinished book of our fraternal "Fioretti," wherein so many hands have written, we shall find some beautiful individual results.

2. Viewing the successes of the whole, we call to mind the fifteen centuries of religious life already lived— the millions of religious who have gone forward in

fraternal union toward the beauty and grandeur to which
God has called them.

We can call to mind, finally, the multitude of saints who
have gone up from our ranks and who will tell us of the
welcome which the Supreme Judge has reserved for His
faithful servants.

I. INDIVIDUAL SUCCESSES

We are sometimes astonished at the extraordinary
patience and meekness of certain people, the discovery of
their consideration, of their knowledge deepened and assimilated by mercy. We sometimes forget that they carry in their
hearts an inexhaustible source of kindness, sweetness, and
sympathy.

One of the most exalted histories, that of the human soul
in its innumerable individual triumphs, will never be written. A professional man has said that the above-mentioned
work would have very little chance of success:

> "Holy people, one doesn't know why, appear to historians
> and their readers in general less interesting than other
> people." [4]

Conscience

To restore confidence in the grandeur and strength of
the human soul, it would suffice to be able to explore the
consciences of a chosen number of the many religious dispersed throughout the world.

"The spirit of a man is the lamp of the Lord searching through his inmost being." [5]

Those sincerely poor (and they are in the majority) have been able to extinguish all desires for wealth even in the presence of enormous sums so tempting to a goodly number of others.

"The law of Thy mouth is more precious to me than mountains of gold and silver." [6]

It is not these simple and upright hearts that need a long commentary on the words of Holy Scripture:

"If thou wouldst have given me a thousand pieces of silver, I would not lay my hands upon the King's son (Absalom)." [7]

Oh, the grandeur of the human conscience! All is settled under the eye of God alone. This is absolute, constant, and delicate fidelity. The least actions as well as the greatest are inspired by the same ardent love without any spirit of vanity or without the hope of an earthly recompense. Because the heart is solidly anchored in compassion and forbearance, one refrains from judging servants "whose eyes are fixed on the hands of their masters." [8] Such a one has ceased to show displeasure to all who look for recompense or indemnity, and to those who live only in the hope of recognition. Those with delicate consciences do not judge, even in their hearts, those who give up work as soon as they are not watched or supervised.

Oppressive overwork, undermined health, and shortened

lives are no longer taken into consideration by hearts committed to rectitude. Certain duty, dictated by conscience, is "the lamp of the Lord." For some months a religious nurse has been watching near a sick person who is doomed and given up by the doctors.[9] In the profound silence of sleepless nights, with ampoules of narcotics or sedatives at hand, this religious is "free" to administer dosages without being checked. But the idea would never enter her mind to cut short, even for a minute, that life, humanly speaking, so useless.

Patience and self-control

It is indeed a triumph for a certain number to have at last acquired mildness. In lives spent in charitable works like those of the greater part of religious vowed to the apostolate, all is sacrificed to the welfare of others, without withdrawal or regret. Days begin whose calls of duty cannot possibly be foreseen. Days go by spent in the dispensaries of poor areas, or in visiting the sick or the afflicted. The length of the visit depends on the needs and on the hopes of the unfortunate. What is the use of wishing to help them if we disappoint their expectations?

Because they are women and of this generation, these religious might wish to read, to develop themselves, to get away from the turmoil. The pitiless rounds of duty seize and entangle them. In seeking to escape, these apostles would have the feeling of betraying souls at a time when God has chosen them to be His messengers of mercy.

The unfortunate

Hearts wherein dwells the tenderness of God, cannot

remain insensible to the harrowing appeals, to the sorrowful glances of the constantly renewed crowd which has need of nothing more than kindness. In the never-ending lines, poor beings drift along who begin to deplore their wrong beginnings. They are followed by those unfortunates who, having failed in their examinations, have been forced to renounce the career they had hoped for. Here likewise are to be found in much too great numbers, young people too soon disappointed by life. It sometimes happens that even very good religious are the last to show interest in some who have been rebuffed, humiliated, and dismissed in many ways: writers without readers, and artists who are penniless but still incapable of giving up the only passion of their lives.

In every land, these universal consolers, the good Cyrenians of their brothers in suffering, meet husbands or wives left alone, with many children in their care. These religious know how to be compassionate with the bitterness of parents who failed in their plans for the education of their children. They likewise visit faithfully those that age has isolated and condemned to great solitude. They have the patience to retrace with the latter the sad itinerary of their melancholy and bankrupt lives. They have attained no ideal; they have subdued no passion. These abandoned ones rebel at the depressing realization of never again being able to arouse the interest or the sympathy of anyone. In listening to the recitals cut short by sobs, even weeping themselves, the compassionate visitors thank their Master for having chosen and singled them out to bring the assurance of His fidelity.

Sinners

The apostles know that their work will not be finished

until death. In the wake of the unfortunate come crowds of sinners. The religious reanimates her patience and revives her gentleness to make herself more attentive and merciful to the complaints, the cries, and the avowals of sinners. In their pressing ranks, she finds downtrodden weaklings and those who are discouraged. There are souls there who are sincerely repentant, but who can scarcely believe in the immensity of God's mercy. The humble religious encounters those who have scandalized others, and who in terror re-read the severity of Christ, defender of the helpless and children.[10]

Friend of God, "Whose property is always to have mercy and to spare, and with Whom pardon is an instinct and a need," [11] the holy religious speaks the language and finds the words of the Lord addressed to sinners in the Gospel. The missions of these unwearying consolers make them irreplaceable to their fellowmen whose frailty is seemingly neverending. If these religious disappeared, the immense throng of the unfortunate and sinners would have no one else to whom they could pour out their despair. Who can tell in how many cases religious are the only ones capable of preparing the way for a priest who will absolve the sinner.

Our successes in and through failure or trial

"Unless the grain of wheat dies. . . ." [12]

Ah! if it were only possible to evaluate the precise "accounting" which God has each of our lives!

"Your eyes have seen my actions; in your book they are written." [13]

"One by one thou hast set my tears in thy sight." [14]

The Master Whom we serve surpasses all others. He overlooks nothing that we do for Him. The passing humiliation as well as the final defeat, the fears and anguish, the tears, the drops of blood, all become seeds for sowing in the hands of the heavenly Sower.

You, O religious, may be the humiliated in all ways: you who have failed in your employment, in your teaching charge or your government; you who were accused and could not defend yourselves; you who may die without having been vindicated. It is you of whom it was said:

> "Blessed are you when men . . . speaking falsely, say all
> manner of things against you for My sake. Rejoice and
> be glad, because your reward shall be great." [15]

And you, O blind religious, guided by the walls of your familiar abode, who sometimes kiss the door posts of your blessed prison which you have not left for many decades; you, the sick, the incurable patients in the community infirmary, when you sigh in the morning at the thought of your monotonous days, calling to mind the apparent uselessness of your lives—then it is that you cast into the earth the seeds for the harvest which will wave abundant and triumphant over your forgotten but fruitful graves.

> "Although they go forth weeping, carrying the seed to
> be sown, they shall come back rejoicing carrying their
> sheaves." [16]

As for you, martyrs, who in the course of so many persecutions have mounted hurdle and scaffold, you who were spat upon by the fanatic crowd in which you recognized the children you had loved and the sick whom you had cured, for you a particular beatitude is promised, the same one from which the Apostles of Jesus Christ drew profit:

"They departed, rejoicing that they had been called upon
to suffer disgrace for the name of Jesus." [17]

Success in joy

Thanks to the prodigality as well as the ingenuity of our Divine Friend, the earthly rewards of the religious life are varied. Among the happy outcomes, let us review one of the most humble.

It happens that certain religious experience pride at moving about a crowd of people, dressed in a habit which is very well known and universally respected. In analyzing this sentiment, one can find there a great joy at having given her youth and life to children, to the weak, and to the abandoned. The sisters can be seen escorting the orphans to the fairs, assemblies, patronal feasts, ducasses, or village celebrations, kermesses, however these festivities may be called in the different countries. Look at them, young or in their declining years. In their hearts as well as in their eyes dwells imperishable youth. They look after the children radiantly happy on the merry-go-rounds, excitedly balancing on see-saws, or riding on the miniature railways. They provide thus some of the childish joys for the abandoned children who demand very little.

"Just this year, nuns from the Hospital of Notre Dame de Bon Secours gave their blood in a Red Cross drive and earned baseball tickets for a group of twenty children at St. Antoine's Orphanage, Montreal. The tickets were offered to encourage blood donors and to help meet the weekly target of 3,000 pints." *

Why should they regret not having children of their own flesh, when this sacrifice, sometimes hard to make, but never withdrawn, has made them be the beloved mothers of hundreds of children without home or parents? They participate largely and during all their lives in the inexhaustible love of Christ for the children of men. We have known thousands of these souls, good, kind, and benevolent, who have entered into the Kingdom. They belong to all countries. Grace has worked marvels in them; it has made them alike in their idealism. They understand the Gospel and the virtues of humility and charity in the same identical way. Some have traveled over all the continents and have gone many times around the world. All their many experiences, both complementary and instructive, have made them helpful to all mankind, indulgent to the slow and painful progress of some nations on their way to truth or moral greatness.

II. COLLECTIVE SUCCESSES

There is one sight on earth for which we will never be able to express our admiration. It is the contemplation of its majesty as a whole. The devotees of earthly beauty have become enraptured at the sight of unforgettable landscapes. The hour has come when our cameras will bring us from the sky pictures of the "Face of the Earth." [18] But the photo-

* The Catholic Register (Denver, Colo.) July 7, 1960.

graphs coming closer to the land masses and the great oceans, will reveal to us only a picture taken during the passing moment.[18b]

Artists are never weary of being able to contemplate the fresh colors of the dawn or the flamboyant hues of scores of sunsets reflected in the rose windows of our cathedrals. These short and isolated visions aid them only poorly to revive the complete enchantment and the limitless variations of the light of God created by the genius of our glass makers through fifteen centuries.

We are still more conscious of our failure to evoke the gigantic spiritual victories gained during fifteen centuries of religious life. How could anyone condense into a few pages the long, long past?

It is impossible to make a resume in sixty lines of the majestic spiritual and apostolic triumphs of the world of religious on their way to perfection in the Church of today.

Our languages are too poor to pay proper honor to the multitude of saints who have already gone forth from our ranks. We cannot imagine that great moment of history when the last Judgment will glorify our lives.

The fifteen centuries already past

In the course of our long and grand past, our predecessors have cast over a continent some of the most sumptuous of its monumental adornments. Judgments differ about these beautiful things, following the quality of the observers.

—It is much easier for acheologists and for crowds to admire a monument or ruins than to perceive the progress of souls towards sanctity.

—The religious of today can still evoke the life which animated these venerable structures.

A great artistic past

Religious cherish the right of recalling what it was like one time

> ". . . when architecture as well as all the other arts and sciences were taught only in the great abbeys. The majority of artists were Benedictine monks, and the greatest number of beautiful buildings are the monastic churches or the churches belonging to the abbeys."

These religious architects went through Europe. They made the great pilgrimages: to Rome, to St. James of Compostela, even as far as the Holy Land. "They sometimes brought the style of their province to places far remote," and on their return, they knew how to utilize brillianty their discoveries and their memories.

On the other hand, the most learned researchers find it impossible to evoke that life which, for centuries, gave vitality to these old buildings or these majestic ruins. They lack the necessary records.[20] A whole collection is available to reveal to us "The Daily Life"[21] of the Greeks and Romans, and of epochs less distant in time. Nothing equivalent can be found that would bring to life the monks and cloistered nuns who peopled Monte Cassino, Cluny, Jumieges, and in the sixteenth century, the Carmels of Spain or the monasteries of the Germanic Roman Empire. How can one recreate a day's work spent in the celebrated kitchen of Fontevrault, and in so many others, less vast, more humble, where so many unknown persons lived and sanctified themselves?

Possible reconstructions

The pursuit of an identical end, inspired by the same ideal, and sought for in the same framework is more surely evocative. Religious are still living in the well-built abbeys erected by their predecessors.[22] Some of them are not unmindful of the multiple advantages of a similar setting; but they prefer to recall the spiritual history lived within these old walls.

Humble sisters thank their Master for having called them to these grand "reliquaries," sanctified and consecrated by so much love. A bell, sometimes one which still rings, summoned their predecessors. They receive Communion at the same railing, kneel in the same stalls, enter the same confessionals. The great crucifix, contemporary with olden times, still extends its arms to them. Oh how many accumulated praises rose from under the vaults of the celebrated abbeys where for so long a time and so many times the Office was chanted!

The old buildings, without human history because without great art, are still for us reminiscent of a past full of love. Let us continue to admire masterpieces jealously guarded and protected in the great museums of the world. But when it comes to exploring the beautiful universe of sincere and loving hearts, we know that the commonest hospices of the countryside have been the humble but poorly lighted setting wherein sublimest hours of love have been lived. It is there that very holy souls, interceding for their brethren, sent up to God the appeals which touched Him and made Him soften so many human hearts. Not all true beauty is found in our books or on the canvases of our painters. Our unpublished "Golden Legend" is so much more beautiful that the most inspired of our poets could never tell it.

We know that the incessant dialogue of prayer between the apostles and God is carried on all over the earth. Eloquent and victorious pleas were murmured in the obscure and miserable stairways of the dwellings of the poor, in the cold rooms, and in the great silent parks. After having perceived everywhere so many ineffable echoes and simple renewals of appeals sent up during the course of ages, one is strengthened in the certainty that human beings were constantly, solidly, and tenderly loved by God Who has made His love perceptible to them through the absolute devotion of consecrated souls.

Present-day successes

One of the splendors of the spiritual world, one of the causes of the maternal pride of the Church, is the million religious in the service of God and of a large portion of humanity. It is in these joyous and brotherly unions of the children of all races that one meets the most beautiful, the most devoted, and the most heroic of souls.

Spiritual results

To all those who wonder what can be produced by the permanent and powerful supplication of this great assembly of prayer, we can say with assurance that these souls have drunk deeply at the spring of the beauty of God. They offer and abandon themselves to that power of assimilation, transformation, and transfiguration. This is one of the foundations of our spiritual optimism.

For the benefit of their generation, a million consecrated persons try to reflect as faithful mirrors the multiple aspects of the beauty of God. They prove to all seekers for the ideal, for virtue, and for moral beauty that the Church remains a miracle, that the "dream" of God has been sought for and made a reality down the centuries. Our group maintains and revives among these seekers for God the desire of seeing His Face.

Results in community life

Some envy the peace of the cloister, the privilege of completely surrendered souls. The impressive silence of our quiet homes procures and explains it, in part. But the peace is above all the fruit of the nobility of souls. How could one imagine without having experienced it, the sweetness and the joy of living in contact with scores of persons called together and who, after long years of struggle, relentlessly pursued often even to heroism, have finally succeeded in mastering their passions. Then it is that they become fitted for devotedness, for indulgence, and universal benevolence. The goodness of God so long contemplated by them has put into their hearts that compassionate charity, the flower and fruit of all virtue. Those starved for the ideal at last realize the wish which was so often on their lips at the short lesson of Prime: [23]

"May the Lord direct your hearts in the charity of God, and the patience of Christ." [24]

Apostolic effects

Privileged children of God, we have the impress of practicing all the virtues of the Gospel, sustained by the Church, our Mother. In our hearts (thanks to the solidarity of Christians and the Communion of Saints) are united and brought to fruition the efforts and aspirations of the best of the faithful who are themselves the chosen ones of all human races. We have the advantage and the mission of embodying their mercy, of making efficacious their prayer for the weak and the discouraged. This abundance, pouring forth from all corners of the Christian world, comes back to dwell in our hearts, making our love increase a hundredfold.

To this power rising from Christian people towards the Communities, are added the sheaves daily gathered by educators, nurses, and visitors of all kinds to the advantage of their homes. These are the words which, with few intermediaries, go straight to the heart of God: the artless comments of children, so full of infinite innocence, the noble words of the sick who, conscious of the richness and power of their sufferings, offer them for the afflictions of the world, and never even ask for their own cure. There are also the upsetting words of the afflicted, the resigned words of the lowly, and the courageous utterances of all the foremost leaders of the grandeur of suffering. All these words are formulas which renew a life and tear it away from mediocrity to set it forth on a road which leads to sanctity.

These things are not pious reveries. The beneficiaries are there to make known our victories. Children, abandoned by their own mothers, have found only tenderness and kindness from religious whose voluntary chastity has redoubled and magnified the maternal instinct. Those condemned or repulsed by all have found pleasure again from being near a good sister who never humiliates them and who respects them as the living images of God. The unloved have discovered an understanding which transforms their lives through a love adapted to all adversity.

Entire regions are bettered and made more Christian. The ideal, devotedness, and forgetfulness of self are here much more plentiful than in other places; laughter is more lighthearted, families are happier. This is the apparent and remarkable work of a group of educators, veritable "awakeners of souls." On the plane of formation of human beings, there is an incomparable victory in that wives and mothers become fundamentally Christian, an achievement that the Church desires and awaits. These results renewed through thousands of examples, in the course of thirty or forty years of teaching, have elevated innumerable persons both morally and spiritually in many countries of the world.

The spirit of a hospital nurse "dwells" very pronouncedly in some beings. There are patients who believe in nothing for the future but the universality of harshness, egotism, and narrowness of mind and heart. They have profited for weeks and months by a silent devotion, one which is complete and considerate. The kingdoms of God are enlarged day by day by these blessed attendants, and become far vaster than one might think.

"Blessed are the meek for they shall possess the earth."[25]

It is the sum of complementary breaths of air that make the breeze, so also do the inspirations carry generous souls toward the heights of sanctity where dwell their great predecessors, the men and women whom the Church has pronounced saints. We admire them without reservation, and our simple evocation of them makes us better. We remain optimistic about the work of God. The ideal of perfection offered by Christ, patterned upon the perfection of the Heavenly Father,[26] is an everyday reality. Thousands of religious of all countries have aimed at it and have tried to ascend the mount of perfection offered to their efforts.

III. SANCTITY

"For how can it be known that we, your people, have found favor with you, except by your going with us? Then we, your people, will be singled out from every other people on the earth." [27]

In the universe of supernatural beauty, the supreme victory is that of sanctity. Why should it, varied and magnificent, not flourish among the great throngs of pilgrims, fascinated and attracted by the splendor of God?

Sincere religious carry in their hearts a twofold dream. They never cease to implore God to help them realize personally all the perfection to which He has called them, and avid for the greater glory of God, they ask Him that the sanctity which the Father wills to offer His privileged ones may flourish and come to maturity.

It is the Master, sovereignly free with His gifts, Who chooses His Saints. But the supplications of all Christian souls work together to the development of sanctity in their generation. In this immense fraternal appeal, religious have always had a large part. Their sincere and ardent aspirations have touched the heart of God. The responses from Heaven were those of the Father, Whose almighty power fulfills desires and goes far beyond our most daring dreams. Let us call to mind, in a few lines, some of these answers.

—God has chosen from our ranks, Doctors for His Church.

—He has given us, and through us to so many souls, remarkable guides.

—Christ will proclaim some day, in the sight of men at the last Judgment, the fullness of our spiritual and apostolic triumphs.

1. Doctors of the Church

From among its thirty Doctors, the Church has chosen fourteen, almost one-half, from our religious families.[28] In this divine gift we dare to see the response of a Father to so many appeals, rising from loving hearts towards the Light, the Truth, and an always more profound desire of knowing God.

"Behold the days come, saith the Lord, and I will send forth a famine into the land; not a famine of bread, nor a thirst of water, but of hearing of the word of God." [29]

After having drawn these Doctors deep into the bosom of His Light, after having put into their hearts expressions which clarify, bewilder, and then transfigure lives, God has given them the faculty of luminous exposition. From their explanations and their discoveries in the world of Infinite Truth, they have produced books which have become the starting points towards spiritual advances and renovations.

Saint Teresa of Avila has certainly drawn numerous followers in congregations of women, by writing:

"My most ardent desire would be to see God glorified, and especially by the learned. When we calculate the overwhelming needs of the Church, it is mockery, it seems to me, to be cast down about anything else than this problem. As a consequence, my incessant prayer goes up to God for teachers of doctrine. It is very evident that one single soul, reaching the peak of perfection, burning with a real love of God, will perform on the apostolic plane much more service than a thousand ordinary souls." [30]

The context proves that theological knowledge obtained through the prayer of the humble becomes a source of sanctity in the Church. We have written in another connection:

"The lasting missions of St. Thomas Aquinas, St. Bonaventure, and St. John of the Cross, appear more wonderful and moving since they have been obtained by the petitions of obscure Christians kneeling in poor churches or homes between the tenth and fifteenth centuries." [31]

2. Spiritual Guides

It is a signal grace to find ourselves in the middle of the twentieth century, following our respective vocations, still drawing from the principles codified by St. Benedict at Subiaco, adopted on Alverno by St. Francis of Assisi or at Manresa by St. Ignatius of Loyola. Throughout the Church religious women are constantly pondering on the pages written at the convent of St. Joseph of Avila by St. Teresa, the great Reformer of Carmel, or the STORY OF A SOUL by St. Therese of Lisieux.

Each morning religious receive Communion and meditate in little cells like those in which St. Madeleine Sophie, St. Euphrasie Pelletier, or the Blessed Mother D'Youville died. Many others have meditated and prayed in the infirmary at Nevers where the celebrated Seer of Lourdes expired, murmuring three times: "Pray for me, a poor sinner."

3. At the Last Judgment

On the day when Christ meets risen mankind as Sovereign Judge He will pronounce upon our final successes:

> ". . . And before Him will be gathered all the nations, and He shall separate them, one from another, as the shepherd separates the sheep from the goats." [32]

And that will be the time when the great concourse of religious will come to take their places at the right hand of the Redeemer:

> "After this I saw a great multitude which no man could number, out of all nations and tribes and peoples and tongues." [33]

Because they were unweariedly devoted in their fraternal efforts, there will be legions of them who have heard the blessed words of the universal Rewarder:

> "I was hungry, and you gave Me to eat; I was thirsty and you gave Me to drink; I was a stranger and you took Me in; naked and you covered Me; sick and you visited Me. I was in prison and you came to see Me and made yourself a voluntary companion of my captivity." [34]

CONCLUSION

After one has lived a long time, observed a great deal, and received spontaneous expressions characterized by deep sincerity, he has certainly a right to compare the kinds of love.

Human love is a wonderful thing especially when a sacrament instituted by Christ has sanctified and exalted it. Those faithful to it say that they are incapable of imagining anything better or more beautiful. But of all earthly loves, that of a Mother is the most devoted, the most faithful. According to the testimony of many persons of all ages and all countries, it is the sweetest and the strongest.

But those who have had the advantage of experiencing successively two forms of love, maintain most emphatically that no one can know the Love whose source is God if he has not drunk of it.

On the ocean of the love of which man is capable, God has raised a high and powerful wave. He makes His privileged ones share in the love of the Father for all mankind. To love Incarnate Love better, the chosen ones of each generation have left

". . . father, mother, brothers, sisters, children, lands and house . . ." [35]

country, race, and even life, for our martyrs are counted by millions.

This love, falling from the heart of a God into human hearts, elevates them to a truly divine passion, the love of all mankind:

". . . Man may be merciful to his fellowman, but the Lord's mercy reaches all flesh." [36]

Convinced of these certainties, and beneficiaries of all these great rewards, religious believe with all their strength in the constant timeliness of their mission.

"What would become of the world without religious?" [37] wrote Saint Teresa. Echoing this word of one of the greatest religious women of all times, Pope Pius XII repeated:

> "What would become of the Church without religious women? What would become of the orphans, the aged, the sick, and the afflicted?"

We believe with all our hearts that hatred will never succeed in triumphing over love. The flame lighted by God Himself will never be extinguished.

Knowing better than others the ideal rising up in the hearts of many of our young people, we are convinced that the torch, received from our predecessors, will find hands ready to receive it and to pass it on to generations which await it, and which will be illuminated by its light.

Poitiers, 1960

1 St. Matthew, VII, 17.

2 Deuter., II, 7.

3 Wisdom, VI, 20-21.

4 Louis Madelin.

5 Proverbs, XX, 27.

6 Psalms, CXVIII, 72.

7 II Samuel, XVIII, 12.

8 Psalms, CXXII, 2.

[9] A religious nurse spent 45 nights in succession near a cancer patient.

[10] St. Matthew, XVIII, 6-7; and St. Mark, IX, 42.

[11] **Deus cui proprium est.** "God, whose property it is to pardon . . ." etc.

[12] St. John, XII, 24.

[13] Psalms, CXXXVIII, 16.

[14] Psalms, LV, 9.

[15] St. Matthew, V, 11-12.

[16] Psalms, CXXV, 6.

[17] Acts, V, 41.

[18] **La Face de la Terre,** French title of a book by the great Austrian geologist, E. Suess (1831-1914).

[18b] The world press of September 29, 1959, announced that the earth had been photographed at an altitude of some 17,000 miles.

[19] Camille Enlart, **Manuel d'Archéologie Francaise,** 1902. Vol. I. Arch. Religieuse

[20] The edition A. t'Serstevens of the **Book of Marco Polo.** Albin Michel, 1955, p. 37, points out that ". . . scarcely the hundredth part of the manuscripts of the Middle Ages has come down to us. Wars, revolutions, fires, usage, and above all negligence, have lost all the rest to us."

[21] Published by Hachette, Paris, France.

[22] In one single region in France we can name Poitiers, Angers, Saumur, Craon, Evron, St. Sauveur-le-Vicomte, Valognes, Vitré, Rennes, Saint Jacut-de le Mer, Ploermel, Redon, Saint Gildas de Rhuys. The list is without doubt incomplete.

[23] On January 14 at the beginning of Lent.

[24] II Thess., III, 5.

[25] St. Matthew, V, 4.

[26] St. Matthew, V, 48.

[27] Exodus, XXXIII, 16.

[28] This is the list arranged in chronological order, based on date of death. St. Gregory the Great †604. St. Bede the Venerable †735. St. Peter Damien †1072. St. Anselm †1109. St. Bernard †1153. St. Anthony of Padua †1231. St. Thomas Aquinas †1274. St. Bonaventure †1274. St. Albert the Great †1280. St. John of the Cross †1591. St. Peter Canisius †1597. St. Lawrence Brindisi †1619. St. Robert Bellarmine †1621. St. Alphonsus Liguori †1787.

[29] Amos, VIII, 11.

[30] **Spiritual Relations,** Avila, 1563.

[31] Ronsin, F. X., S.J., **Awakeners of Souls,** Spes, 1955. English translation pub. by Society of St. Paul, Staten Island, N. Y., 1957. p. 296.

[32] St. Matthew, XXV, 32.

[33] Apoc., VII, 9.

[34] St. Matthew, XXV, 35-36.

[35] St. Mark, X, 29.

[36] Sirach, XVIII, 11.

[37] Autobiography, Chap. XXXIII.